Message from the Colonel

by

David Spencer

Dedication

To Martin with my eternal love and gratitude,
and my parents John and Amelia Spencer

David

Published by

Words by Design

www.wordsbydesign.co.uk

ISBN: 978-0-244-60530-8

Copyright © 2004 by David Spencer

Foreword

I first met David in 1969 in Watchet when I joined his Regimental Band from boy service in Sutton Coldfield. However, my time in Watchet was a matter of weeks as I was sent to the Royal Military School of Music in Twickenham, while the band was posted to Berlin. A year later I rejoined the band and began a friendship that has lasted to this day.

My first recollection of David is one of a good musician. He could certainly hold his own in the clarinet section but it was his conducting skills that set him apart. It was very unusual for anyone below the rank of Sergeant to conduct the band, but the bandmaster and those in authority were never in any doubt about his skills or knowledge. It was while the band was stationed in Catterick that I really appreciated how good a conductor he was. He had the advantage of a good musical ear and could easily correct the mistakes made by the musicians. He corrected the faults in a tactful, knowledgeable and professional manner. It was a breath of fresh air not to sit in a band and the only mistakes the conductor could find was that we were too loud!

It must be acknowledged here that David was also a very popular member of the band. For those who are unaware of Army or even band life, one spends a lot of time sitting and waiting around. David could keep our morale up with varied stories and jokes. Regimental band life can also be a 'rat race' as musicians try to earn 'brownie points' in an effort to move up the slow promotion ladder. It is to David's credit that he took no part in this pastime.

It was a sad day when David was posted away and even sadder when we heard he had left the Army and we lost touch.

My wife Rosemary and I were delighted to receive a letter from David in 1995 prior to our posting to Nepal. His news was fantastic and we were delighted to hear about Martin. Over the next couple of years we all became good pen-pals and looked forward to our first meeting. In 1998 we visited them both in Luxembourg and our lasting memory is of a couple who are totally suited to each other, very much in love and have a relationship that is the envy of many couples.

In recent years we have met annually in such places as Munster, Maastricht, Berlin, Amsterdam, Paris and Copenhagen. David and Martin are excellent company and our meetings are one of the first things we plan at the start of each year.

I thank David for his friendship, honesty, integrity and humour. However, above all, I thank him for writing that letter in 1995 and renewing our friendship. Roll on our next meeting in London!

CHRIS DAVIES MBE, Major
Diss, Norfolk

Chris and Rosemary Davies,
outside Buckingham Palace

Contents

Illustration Index

David

'Unto yourself be true.'

On a wet day early in 1975, with the wind howling across the open expanses of this once American air base, now home to the Army's Queen Division, I stood in the corridor outside the Commanding Officer's office and waited. My features were a mask as I tried to hide the fear that ran to my very core. The weather that morning matched my situation perfectly. Wearing my khaki No 2 dress, the white chevrons of my rank stood out on both upper arms, while the ribbon of my General Service Medal added a splash of colour to the dullness of the uniform. As no charges had yet been laid against me, I was allowed to wear my beret, with its distinctive red and white hackle (plume) of the Royal Regiment of Fusiliers. All around me, clerks and orderlies scurried, their eyes averted, giving me a wide berth. It was as if I had a contagious disease and they wanted to do everything that they could to avoid the contagion. I had never felt so lonely in my life. My whole world had collapsed around me as my worst nightmare had finally come true. The fear that had haunted me for the past twelve years had at last caught up with me. And it was all my own fault. I'd inflicted a huge, gaping wound on myself, in an act of the most extraordinary madness – or was it desperation?

Almost thirty years later, I now know the answer. In a way it was a huge relief. All the years of hiding, guilt, and self-hate had finally taken their toll and if I had to serve some time in the glass-house for it to finally come to an end, then so be it.

I was at the literal end of my tether and could take no more. What was my crime? I was a homosexual and my guilty secret was out in the open, for everyone to see.

The Regimental Sergeant Major stood facing me, his boots gleaming, while his eyes looked at me from beneath the peak of his cap, his face empty of emotion. If he had any thoughts, he hid them well.

"RSM," the CO's voice called from his inner sanctum.

"Sir," answered the Sergeant Major as he marched towards the door, his boots clicking on the highly polished tiled floor. There was the murmur of voices for a few seconds, before the RSM reappeared, and looked in my direction. "The CO will see you now, Corporal Spencer," he said, not unkindly. I was surprised. I wasn't to be marched in at double time, like a prisoner. They'd spared me that indignity, at least for the time being. I came to attention and marched into the large, spacious office, my eyes focused just above the colonel's head. Bringing my right leg down sharply I came to attention and saluted. The CO was a fusilier, like myself, which somehow made my ordeal even worse. For a few seconds he ignored me, before slowly raising his eyes and looking at me, his face full of loathing. I could expect no compassion from this man. He looked me up and down, as if something slimy had suddenly appeared in front of him. With a look of distaste he said, quietly, and ominously, "Spencer. If I can crucify you, then I will. Now get out!"

I said, "Yes, Sir," feeling like a homosexual must have felt standing before his tormentors, in their jet black uniforms, some forty years previously. I make no apologies for using this comparison. No, they weren't going to put me inside a gas chamber, but if they could, they would certainly destroy me and leave me hanging for the whole world to see. Coming to attention, I saluted, about-turned and marched out.

The RSM was waiting. "Come into my office," he said, quietly, as I followed him down the corridor, entered his office and closed the door. He sat down and faced me, probably the most powerful man in any regiment, after the CO. RSM's in the British Army have a fearsome reputation which they cultivate and have honed down to perfection over the years. Any soldier with an ounce of common sense avoids the RSM like the plague. In reality, of course, they are highly intelligent men with many years of service and experience behind them. He gave a sigh as he looked at me. "You really are a bloody fool, Corporal Spencer. You've thrown it all away. No matter what happens now, your Army career's finished," he said, quietly. "Anyway, it's much too late now. You're under investigation by the SIB." (The Criminal Investigation Branch of the Royal Military Police.) I already knew that, as they had interviewed me in the guardhouse the previous day. He continued, "If they can prove a case against you, you do realise that you can expect a court-marshal, and, if you're found guilty, a spell in Colchester, followed by a dishonourable discharge?" "Yes, Sir," I murmured almost inaudibly.

"As it is," he continued, "For the moment, no charges have been laid against you. The SIB investigation into your activities is ongoing, and you'll be informed of any charges in due course. For the moment, you're to be transferred to the KAPE team (Keep the Army in the public eye), under Major 'C'." He looked at me with something like compassion, as he said, "Listen to me, Corporal Spencer. I've been in this man's army for many years now, and you're not the first homosexual that I've ever come across. In my time, I've attended the military funerals of a number of men like you. I do not, I repeat, do not, want to attend yours. Do you understand?" I nodded, and said, "Yes, Sir." "Very well, off you go."

I about-turned and marched out of the office as his eyes bored into my back. I hurried out into the daylight and almost ran back to my room. As I shut the door behind me, huge sobs began to wrack my body and tears that had been held back for years streamed down my face, the thought of suicide very real in my mind. The music had at last reached a crescendo, but the finalé was still a long way off.

Childhood

I came on the scene on 20ᵗʰ March 1948, at 136 Church Street, in the district of Lozells, Birmingham, the third child of John and Millie Spencer. We were a working class family and Dad worked at the *Joseph Lucas* factory, where he'd been employed throughout the war years. We weren't poor, but I imagine that money was tight. The family never went without, and there was always plenty of food on the table and decent clothes on our backs. My first real memory is of a joyous occasion, the Coronation of Queen Elizabeth II in June 1953. I remember it as if it were yesterday. A cold and wet day, but that didn't deter the street celebrations to welcome in the new 'Elizabethan Era'. Bunting was everywhere as the good citizens of Church Street gave joyous voice and wore fancy dress. I was Sir Francis Drake, dressed in a little pair of yellow pantaloons and some bobbles tied with elastic around a pair of pumps, proudly carrying a plastic sword, and wearing a ruff of multicoloured crepe paper. Sadly I couldn't stay awake for long enough to see out the celebrations and fell asleep, half frozen to death on the back of a lorry. However, I did wake up for long enough to join the fancy dress parade and tuck into the abundance of fish-spread sandwiches, jelly and lemonade.

The houses in Church Street were of much better quality than the back-to-backs that had been my mother's childhood home. However don't let that fool you, as none of them had bathrooms or inside toilets. At least we didn't have to share and used proper toilet rolls, unless we ran out, and then it was back to *The Evening Mail*. These houses were known as tunnel-backs, and most of the Lozells area consisted of this type of housing, built in the late nineteenth century for the 'artisans' and blue collar workers of the city. The row of houses was continuous, with a covered entry leading to the back and giving access to the gardens and rear entrances, one on the left and one on the right. The gardens were long and narrow, a privet hedge usually dividing the garden from its neighbour. At the end of our garden, Dad and my brother John built a large shed with a veranda at the front and a closed-in back. I was to put that shed to good use in later years. As you entered through the back gate, you faced the door that led into a large kitchen, with a scullery to the right, and a door to the left leading into the living room. If you walked through the living room, at the end on the right was a door going out into a narrow hallway with the stairs to the upper floor on the right; on the left was a door into the best room which had a window overlooking the street. The front door was at the end of the hall.

The Spencer family, about 1953
John, John, David, Millie and Christine

At the top of the stairs was a small bedroom; as you turned right there was another room facing you, and at the end of a hallway a large bedroom that looked out onto the street below. Luxury indeed, eh? My sister, Christine, had the small room at the back, I shared the middle room with my brother, John, and Mom and Dad had the front bedroom. There was a quite large attic at the top of the house, which was never used, except by me as a den. I remember how cold those rooms could be in winter, and very often we covered the bed with an old army greatcoat for extra warmth. For calls of nature, if you needed a pee in the middle of the night, you could use the chamber pot strategically placed under the bed. For anything else, it was a case of putting on your overcoat and going out into the back yard to the toilet. That was no joke on a bitterly cold night in the middle of January. I remember that Dad and a plumber friend installed a bathroom in the old scullery sometime in the mid 1950s. We must have been the first family in the street to enjoy the luxury of being able to take a bath at any time just by turning the tap. This house, No 136, was my home from my birth until I left school.

School Days

Aged 5, I started at Anglesey Street primary school, just around the corner, a two-minute walk away. I remember my first teacher to be a shrivelled old harridan called Miss Evans, who seemed ancient even then. One day she caught me with my hand up my shorts, as little boys sometimes do. She called me a dirty, disgusting little boy. A look of horror flashed across her face as she showed Victorian disapproval. I bet that she hated little children, and boys in particular. Mrs Angel, on the other hand, was a lovely Welsh woman, who lived up to her name. On many occasions she called me to the front of the class, passed me a note, and asked me to take it around to my mother. It all seemed very strange to me as I was supposed to be doing my lessons, but I dutifully ran home and gave the note to Mom, who nodded and said, "Tell Mrs Angel that that's alright." After school, Mrs Angel would come around carrying a large bag and Mom would fill it with coal! I realise now that the poor woman had a serious drink problem leading to money worries. What happened to her I don't know, but she's someone that will stay in my memory forever.

Even to this day, I shudder whenever I hear the hymn, *In the bleak mid winter*. We used to sing it at morning assembly, and it will always remind me of my early school days and my struggle with arithmetic, which I still carry with me to this day. I suspect that I was mildly dyslexic, something unheard of in those dim and distant days. It would explain a lot.

Saturday night was 'pop and sweet' night, when Dad would give me two shillings and I would run up to the tobacconist, newsagent and sweet shop, *Mr Wallace's*, on the corner of Church Street and Burbury Street. Mr Wallace was a miserable sour-faced man, whom everyone suspected of being pro-Nazi during the war. What a delight that shop was to a little boy, with shelves full of jars of sweets, chocolate bars and crates of pop. My favourite drink was *Tizer*, and I would buy a large bottle and a selection of sweets that Mr Wallace would weigh out on a little set of scales. Dad had a bill there, and would have the newspaper, our comics and his cigarettes, *Player's No 6*, put down in the book. He'd settle up at the end of the week, when he'd been paid. When I was older, I'd often go into the shop and get a packet of cigarettes 'for Dad'. In fact they were for me (I started young), and fortunately I never got caught out. After getting my Saturday night treat, I'd disappear down to our Violet's at number 150 and spend the evening with her watching television while George went up the pub. I adored Vi, such a good woman. She was of course my mother's aunt, and I always called her Auntie Vi, but more of her later.

Another favourite shop was *Uncle's*. It was at the other end of the road, on the corner of Burbury Street and Anglesey Street, and was owned by a woman called Dolly Richards, who was a friend of Mom's. Uncle was her brother, a nice man who was stone deaf and we kids had to shout at the top of our voices to make him hear. Dolly treated the poor chap worse than a dog, and was forever shouting at him. *Uncle's* was a grocery shop, but the attraction for us youngsters was the frozen 'Jubblies', an orange drink put into the fridge and turned into a large, strangely-shaped iced lollypop. After school we'd troop in there to by our Jubblies and devour them on the way home.

On Saturday morning, Mom, Vi and I would walk up to what was known as 'The Flats'. They were a row of shops in Lodge Road, Hockley. We'd first go to the butcher's on the corner of

Heaton Street and Lodge Road and buy the meat for the
Sunday roast, together with some delicious home-made
sausages that we always had for Saturday dinner with creamy
mash and thick gravy. Then it was across the road to
Woolworth's to buy some broken biscuits, tea and various
other things at knock-down prices needed for the week ahead.
And then it was David's treat time. On the corner of Spring
Hill was a large department store; I think it was called *Kay's*.
We'd go to the cafeteria on the top floor and I'd have a round
of toast with a banana milk-shake, while Mom and Vi had a
cup of tea, and then it was back home.

David in about 1954

Church Street was well served for local shops. If you walked down the street and turned left into Nursery Road, you would find on the left a row of shops. Firstly there was *Robinson's* the newsagents. I remember Mr Robinson well, a tall, stiff-backed man who looked like a retired colonel. I was more than a little scared of him. Violet would buy her weekly supply of snuff from there. Next was *Bartlet's* the butcher, followed by *Beech's* fish and chip shop. Mr Beech was nearly always drunk, as he spent most of his time in the pub on the corner of Villa Street and Nursery Road. Next to them was a grocery store that sold faggots and peas on a Friday night, and lastly a sweet shop, owned by an old, half-blind lady, whose name I forget. Nursery Road was the main thoroughfare and on the No 8 bus route. On many evenings I'd run down from home and wait at the bus stop to meet my dad coming home from work. Just by the bus stop, on the corner, was *Bert's* the greengrocers. With all these shops a housewife could do all of her shopping without going far from home. This was of course in the days before supermarkets. Our milk was still delivered by horse-drawn milk float. Tommy, the bread man who called every morning, was often late because he had a habit of stopping for a half-pint at every pub on his round, and was often pretty sozzled when he arrived. He was a nice chap, but I believe he was sacked when he arrived one Friday afternoon to collect his money, the worse for drink, and a householder complained.

I can't overestimate the part that dear Violet played in my young life. It's a sad fact that we never really appreciate the people that we love until it's too late. I spent as much time with her at 150 Church Street as I could, which tells you something I think. I'd rush home from school and go down to Violet's. Dad had found them the house during the war. He often said, with some justification, that George Brookes was incapable of doing anything for himself. Vi would boil me an egg, and we'd sit in front of the fire and make toast. I'd then sit and watch 'Children's Hour' on the television. During the school holidays I'd go down and help her with the washing on

22

Monday mornings. Believe it or not, she was still using an old-fashioned boiler in the 1950s. It was a brick structure with a fire-grate underneath. Filled by a bucket of water from the tap, you lit the fire and waited for the water to boil. Afterwards, she'd use an equally old-fashioned mangle to extract the excess water and hang the washing all out to dry. George was so tight, that I remember her having to use an iron that she heated on the fire to do the ironing.

There's a lovely story, which shows the incredible neighbourliness of the times. On the morning that Vi and George moved into 150, their next door neighbour, Mrs Jones, took around a large jug of tea. Not to be outdone, Vi returned the compliment. This daily ritual was to carry on right up until Vi died in the early 60s.

Thursdays was cleaning day at 136, and Vi and her sister Ada would descend on the house and get busy helping Mom. They would polish and dust, empty the chamber pots and generally bustle round, continually falling over each other.

Ada was also a lovely woman, as were all of the Jukes sisters, my mother's aunts. She was only partially sighted, but had the most bubbly personality, and bore her handicap with incredible fortitude. She was always singing and laughing and loved me to bits. Her husband, George, was totally blind. He'd been married before and had a son, Stanley, who died tragically of a heart attack at a very young age. They lived in a council house in Weoley Castle. I remember one sunny day walking from Church Street all of the way to Weoley Castle to visit them with my sister Christine and some friends. It was a long walk, but in those days, it was still safe for young children to roam the streets.

On Saturday mornings I'd often forgo the pleasure of my milkshake for a trip to the pictures at Aston Cross. It cost sixpence to get in and was absolute bedlam, with kids running about causing chaos and mayhem. We'd watch our heroes Hoppalong Cassidy and Roy Rodgers, with the weekly Flash Gordon adventure always finishing with a nail biting end, making sure that you would come back next week to see what happened. Because I was so young, I'd go with my older sister, Christine, and her friend Pauline Jones, who lived next door to Vi. Some of the older children were monitors, who tried to keep order and wore a special armband. Some hope!

George would sometimes come home from the pub after closing time on Saturday afternoon, have his dinner, belch, say "Manners," and decide to visit his mother and father in Curdworth near to Tamworth. As I spent as much time as I possibly could at Violet's, I was almost always there when George made his announcement, and would of course be invited along. I jumped at the chance, as it was always an adventure. We'd walk to Hockley Brook and take the bus up to Snow Hill Station, then stroll through the centre of the town and down to the Bull Ring. We'd go into the market, where George would buy a plate of whelks and swallow the lot, before we proceeded to catch the *Midland Red* bus to Tamworth.

George's parents always seemed incredibly old to me. His mother was a tiny, shrivelled woman, with a wrinkled face. She always reminded me of a gypsy as she invariably wore a knitted shawl. His father, whom I called Uncle Billy, must have been a tall man in his youth, but was by now stooped with age. He'd served in the British Army, and had been at the siege of Mafeking during the Boer War. They were always pleased to see me, and would insist on giving me a kiss, but I didn't really mind as they were so nice and kind to me. After a while, we'd walk through the village to see George's sister, Flossie, and her husband (I don't remember his name). Their son, Victor, who was a lot older than me, would take me across the fields to play on the swings. As the evening approached I'd start to get excited, as I knew that it would soon be time for a trip to the pub, before our return to Birmingham.

I wasn't of course allowed into the *White Swan*, but was quite content to stand outside and be fed a diet of *Vimto* and crisps until the bus arrived to take us back to Birmingham. We'd jump off the *Midland Red* at Aston Cross, and get onto the No 8 bus. George would get off at the top of Nursery Road and go into his local to finish the night off, while Vi and I would carry on to the next stop. The pub was a place that I would frequent a lot myself in the years to come. George and I later became drinking partners – much to the disgust of my mother – and would spend many hours in this den of iniquity. Vi would stop by her front door and watch me run up the hill, safely home, a tired but very happy little boy.

Sundays were a different story, and church was on the menu. Mom worshipped at Saint Saviour's, on the corner of Villa Street and Bridge Street. We both sang in the choir at morning service, and again during the evening. I also had to go to Sunday school in the afternoons, and would very often sing at weddings on a Saturday afternoon. For that we were paid the princely sum of one shilling. I had a very beautiful soprano voice (even though I say it myself), and was head choirboy. When St Saviour's was closed down, we moved to St Silas's at the top of Church Street. By that time my voice had broken and I was let loose with the other older boys and girls. We always sat at the very back of the church, as far away from the adults as possible.

Mom has been a practising Christian all of her life; I think that the dreadful experiences of her early days made her turn to the church. That's not to say that she's a saint, far from it. I believe that her upbringing, the fact that she lost her father and was abandoned by her mother, made her very bitter, and she has carried that bitterness with her throughout her life. There is no doubt, however, that her beliefs are genuine, and they have been a great source of comfort to her. My relationship with her has always been difficult and fraught with a bitterness of my own. A dear friend and relative recently said to me, "You always seemed the outsider, Dave." I think that there's a lot of truth in that.

My mother's childhood was in many ways an unhappy one and perhaps some of it should be mentioned here. It's impossible for me to tell the story in great depth, but I'll try to give you some idea of her background.

Mom was born in January of 1915 in a back-to-back house in Ladywood, a working class district of Birmingham. Her father, Walter, enlisted in the army along with thousands like him at the outbreak of war in August 1914. Serving with the Kings Royal Rifle Corps, he saw extensive action on the western front. Mom's brother was conceived during a leave from France, a leave that was to be Walter's last. Walter had a premonition of his death and seriously considered deserting, but was dissuaded by his father-in-law, John Jukes. On the night that he was due to return to the front, he went out and got drunk, swearing that he wouldn't go and "To hell with it." After Walter plunged his bayonet into the parlour door in a fit of rage, John Jukes calmed him down. Turning to John, known by everyone as 'Pop', he said quietly, "Pop, will you promise me one thing?"
"Of course, son," replied the old man.
"Look after Millie and the kids when I'm gone."
"Yes, Wal, I promise," said the old man.
The next day the family saw Walter for the last time as he boarded the train and left for France and his death.

In April 1917, during the latter stages of the battle of Arras, Walter was badly wounded. He was taken to the military hospital in Rouen, where he died on the 18th. He was laid to rest in the military cemetery, a place of great beauty and tranquillity. Walter was just 24 years old when he died. I took my mother to Rouen in 1995 to see his grave for the first time. She was in her 80th year and had revered her father's memory all of her life.

Mom's brother, named Walter after his father, was born in 1917. The two children were brought up by their mother and lived with their grandfather, Pop, and his wife, Amelia, in Ladywood. Pop had a large family – they were a typical working class family of that period and times were hard for everyone. Mom's mother was the eldest girl, followed by Emma, Violet, Ada and a boy called Jack.

Emma had the misfortune to get pregnant while unmarried and Pop threw her out. That was the way of dealing with those circumstances at that time. She was forced to marry the father, who was called Albert Faulkner, a drunk, wife-beater and womaniser. Poor Emma had the worst life of them all, taking cleaning jobs wherever she could to make ends meet. Her life was a round of babies, drudgery and violent abuse with never enough food on the table. Albert would get her pregnant and disappear for weeks on end with some fancy woman. On his return the cycle would repeat itself over and over again. His children trudged around the streets of Birmingham, pushing a hand-made cart and selling bundles of firewood to try to make a few coppers. At one point, when Emma was pregnant yet again, the children had to go into a children's home while she was sent to the workhouse so that she could have the baby. The family was reunited shortly after the new arrival had been born. The children would often sit in their bedroom killing the bugs and vermin over a candle flame. On many nights, they would sit cowering at the bottom of the stairs, while their mother was given a drunken beating over some imagined slight, the remains of an uneaten meal lying in the fire-grate, where it had been thrown in a drunken rage. They were always hungry, with often not a crust in the house.

I have the greatest respect for Emma, a woman of courage and dignity who loved her children and was much loved by them in return. Sadly, I only vaguely remember her. After her legal separation from Albert in December of 1940, life was better for her and she went on to live a happy and long life. Although still a young woman when she separated, she never looked at another man again.

Her daughter, Edie, I hold in the highest esteem. It's with my eternal gratitude and love that I give my thanks to her for her help and the invaluable information that she's passed on to me about those hard times.

The third of Pop's daughters, Violet, I loved dearly and remember my childhood days spent with her with great affection. Sadly, there's not enough room here for me to detail her life. She was a lovely woman who always smothered me with love and I'll always be indebted to her. Her life was an unhappy one with a loveless marriage.

Violet Brookes, nee Jukes, was ever present throughout my early years and into adolescence. I can still see her now, all of these many years later, wearing her wrap-around pinafore and taking a surreptitious pinch of snuff from time to time. When she was tired, she'd sit in the kitchen on an upright chair, her stockings unfastened from her suspender belt and hanging around her ankles. I think that she would have loved children of her own, but sadly, that was not to be. When she died in 1965, I attended the funeral wearing my No 1 dress uniform. As the cortege pulled away, the curtains of the surrounding houses were closed as a mark of respect. A man, obviously an old soldier, slowly came to attention as we passed by. My heart was heavy that day. Perhaps Violet Brookes represented the grandmothers that I never knew, I don't know. What I can say is this, dear Aunt Violet will forever remain in my memory. Her passing marked the end of my childhood and the start of my own journey.

Violet's sister, Ada, was a woman of incredible courage and fortitude who faced her blindness with humour. I remember her when I was a child, always laughing and joking and never seeming to mind her disability. Like Violet, she always treated me with great kindness.

Pop's son, Jack, was a strange little man who frightened me with his rough, working class 'Brummie' ways. Jack spent the war years in the Pioneer Corps. This regiment often had to perform some of the most ghastly jobs imaginable, like burying the dead, and he saw some terrible sights. He would often turn up at Violet's house after the pubs had closed on a Saturday afternoon. I can still smell his 'beery' breath to this day. He was never unkind and would sometimes give me half-a-crown (2/6), but I was always just a little frightened of him.

My grandmother, Amelia, I never knew. I do, however, know a lot about her. Still a young woman after her husband's death in 1917, and with two small children to bring up, she lived with her father and mother. Pop was a well-respected member of the community and very upright in his behaviour. A life-long Conservative, he worked for the *New Hudson Cycle Company,* and served behind the bar of the 'Snug' at the *Shakespeare* public house in Ladywood. It was Pop who brought up my mother and her brother Walter, teaching them to respect the memory of their father and the sacrifice that he'd made. Each November 11th he would take the children to the hall of memory in Broad Street for the service of remembrance. Pop kept the promise that he had made to his son-in-law in 1917 and looked after the children. It's just as well that he did.

I've known the tragic story of my grandmother's death in 1929 for over 40 years. In fact, it's become almost folklore and taken on the aspect of a fairy tale, something not quite believable, or in some way exaggerated. I decided to get to the truth once and for all, but where to start? We live in the

29

electronic age and almost anything is possible, just by turning on the computer, which is what I did. First I decided that I needed a copy of the death certificate and contacted the registrar of births, marriages and deaths in Birmingham. Sure enough, for the payment of £7, I was able to obtain a copy. I didn't even need to lift the telephone, sending all of the details by e-mail and receiving a reply within a week.

The envelope landed on the mat one bright but cold morning in early October. I sat down and opened it. Let me tell you, hearing a story is one thing, seeing the evidence in black and white is quite another. The words seemed to jump up at me from the paper and hit me in the face with force, making me gasp. For the first time in my life I felt real compassion for my mother and a lot of unanswered questions were finally answered, at least in my mind. At last the jigsaw was beginning to come together and make a whole.

At the time of her husband's death in April 1917, Amelia Smith was only 24 years old, still a young woman. My mother was less than 2½, whilst Walter hadn't even been born. It should be remembered, however, that thousands upon thousands of women found themselves in exactly the same position, and had to cope as best they could. Amelia was awarded a war widow's pension and, I believe, lived with her mother and father, Pop and Amelia in St Mark's Street.

It's not clear exactly when she met Ernest McCarthy and moved in with him. I do know, however, that she and her cousin Ada Inscoe, daughter to Amelia's mother's sister, Emma, spent evenings out together at the Aston Hippodrome, a well-known music hall of the day. It was there that my grandmother met Ernest one evening – but there was a problem. Ernest was already married and was in no position to offer Amelia marriage, even if she'd wanted it. Whether Ernest left his wife to set up home with Amelia, or whether he was already separated from his wife, I have no way of knowing. They started to live together as man and wife. It would have been impossible for them to be openly cohabiting together, given the mores of the time, and Ernest became Mr Smith.

The word 'abandoned' is an emotive one, but Amelia left her children, Walter and Millie, in the care of her parents. For myself, I think that Amelia's decision was purely a practical one. She was in receipt of a government pension, and had the authorities discovered the true situation, she would have lost it, something that she could ill afford to do. I do know that she paid some of it towards the up-keep of the two children. Young Walter tells a story that, one day, Pop spied an inspector from the local authority coming up the yard and told him to hide under the table, as he shouldn't have been there. Walter tells his own story in great detail later on in this book, and gives us a good insight to his life growing up in Birmingham in the years following the First World War.

I do know that Amelia had her first child by Ernest in 1923. She was called Evelyn and was followed by a son, Leonard. I know absolutely nothing of the life that they led during those years and won't speculate. Ernest was a bricklayer and therefore a skilled tradesman, whilst Amelia was a brass polisher by profession.

My mother comes into the story some years later, at around the age of 14 or 15. For some reason, she went to live with her mother and Ernest. She has often claimed that Ernest was treating Amelia badly and her mother asked her to go and stay with her, in the hope that this would curb him. However, I think that this story should be treated with some caution. From people who knew Ernest and are still living today, the impression is given that he wasn't a bad man. Never having known him, I'm in no position to judge.

I do know that Mom had to travel to school, there and back everyday, from their address at No 12, Apollo Row in, I think, Selly Oak, to her school in St Mark's Street – a long journey. However, the events that followed are indisputable.

One afternoon, on September 24th 1929, my mother came home from school. She found her mother lying on the bed slowly bleeding to death. Mom rushed to get help and an ambulance was called. As Amelia lay there, she whispered to Mom, "Millie, forgive me." Amelia Smith died later that night in Selly Oak Hospital – she was 35 years old. What caused her death? The poor woman died of a back-street abortion that went badly wrong. In the cold, clinical medical terms of the death certificate, the cause of death is given thus: 'Post Partum Haemorrhage, Abortion, three months gestation.' After a post mortem without inquest, the coroner for Birmingham, W H Davison, signed the certificate. The informant is given as Violet Brookes, sister of the deceased and residing at 35, Dixon Road, Small Heath.

In those days, back-street abortion was common - too many mouths to feed and not enough money to go around. Amelia took to her grave her reason for what she did. The story made none of the Birmingham newspapers and no one was ever charged with any crime. I heard that a woman who owned a local shop was known to the police as an abortionist and was suspected by them, but that's just hearsay. I'm beginning to think that Amelia induced the abortion herself and that no one else was involved. No inquest was ever held, only the post-mortem, which would suggest that the coroner could find no evidence of any crime being committed. If he had have done, then he would have recorded a verdict of unlawful killing and the police would have investigated.

Mother sat on the doorstep and waited until the early hours of the morning for her mother to come home. She waited in vain. It's reputed that a policeman arrived and saw her sitting there. He asked her where her father was, and she replied, "He's not my father, but he's upstairs in bed." "Go and fetch him," said the policeman, and Mother obeyed. Ernest came down, dishevelled and half-asleep. The policeman looked at him, grabbed hold of his pyjama jacket at the throat and hissed,

"Your wife is lying dead in the hospital, and you're lying upstairs in bed, you bastard!"

Within days of Amelia's death, her mother suffered a massive stroke, no doubt bought on by her daughter's tragic death. She died on October 29th 1929 aged 57. The two women, mother and daughter were both laid to rest in Yardley cemetery, two funerals within a month.

I have a photograph of my mother and young Walter taken outside the house in St Mark's Street on the day of their mother's funeral. Mom is dressed in a new outfit and wearing a fashionable cloche hat, whilst poor old Walter is still dressed in his ragged clothes. Violet had bought the new outfit for Mom out of some insurance money. Sadly, there was not enough to be able to buy two outfits, so Walter had to do without. The day of his mother's funeral was, incidentally, Walter's 12th birthday.

And what of Ernest McCarthy? There is absolutely no evidence to suggest that he had any knowledge of what Amelia planned to do. It's entirely possible that he didn't even know that she was pregnant. Only he could answer that question and, like Amelia, he took the answer with him to his grave. For myself, I refuse to speculate.

Let's sit back for a moment and reflect on the terrible effect that this dreadful incident must have had on my mother. The psychological trauma that she suffered that day must have been enormous, and I believe that she's carried the scars inflicted on her at that time, right up until the present day. No child should be forced to witness the horror that she undoubtedly saw on that day in 1929. Remember she was just 15 years old, and there was no such thing as counselling in those far off days, whilst post traumatic stress disorder syndrome wasn't understood or even known about, and wouldn't be for a very long time to come, far too late to help my mother. She must have suffered and suffered alone.

Mom has always revered the memory of both her mother and father. To Mom, Amelia has taken on the persona of a saint, and in her mind her mother could do no wrong. Of course Amelia was no saint, none of us are, and we should remember the biblical passage, "Let he amongst you who is without sin, cast the first stone." No, my grandmother was a human being with all of the faults and frailties that we all share. In the end she paid a fearful price and I hope that she's resting in peace. As for Ernest, my mother (rightly or wrongly) has loathed him for most of her life and lays the blame for her mother's death firmly at his door. However, I for one do not believe that he's as bad as has been painted.

'Friday Night is Music Night.' Do you remember that BBC radio programme? It was broadcast at 9.00 pm on Friday evenings and Dad loved it. He was a musician, and would sit in the kitchen of No 136, listening avidly to the light classical music being broadcast. As a little boy I would often sit with him and wave my arms around like a conductor. He'd stand me on a chair, give me one of Mom's knitting needles and encourage me to conduct. It was almost as if he knew that one day I would stand in front of real musicians and conduct them. He was right, but more of that later. The children were all encouraged to learn to play the piano, although I showed no interest – it's ironic that I would go on to be a musician myself and make a living at it. I believe that the seeds of my love of music were planted in those days.

Childhood Christmas was an exciting time, waking very early in the morning and finding a pillowcase full of presents at the end of the bed. I would take them into Christine's bedroom and we'd open them together. It was she who one year told me that there wasn't really a Father Christmas. I don't recall being too bothered, just as long as the presents kept coming.

Dad was no fool, and taught me a lesson that's lasted me my whole life. When I was about nine, I had this fascination with the Nazis; it wasn't that long after the horrors of the Second

World War.   Of course, I was only a child, and didn't understand.   I think the attraction was the uniforms and martial music (I love German marches to this day).   I was forever going around the house shouting "Heil Hitler," and it must have been galling for someone who'd been through those terrible times.   One evening he announced that I could stay up and watch a programme on the television.   I was excited, what a treat, being allowed to stay up in the middle of the week.   I was in for a shock, which of course was the intention.   It was a documentary about the Nazi death camps, and I was horrified by the scenes that I saw that night.   I've seen those images many, many times since then, and my loathing of extremism of any sort was born.   It took me a long time to get to sleep that night, and I never again said, "Heil Hitler."

This would be a very good point in the saga to talk a little about Mom and Dad as I was growing up.   While we never suffered the poverty of my mother's childhood, money was, I imagine quite tight at times.   Dad was a working man with a young family to bring up, and being old-fashioned, would never let Mom go out to work.   He believed that it was his job to bring in the money, and Mom's to bring up the family.   It wasn't until many years later that Mom almost literally sneaked out of the house and found herself a job in Birmingham's 'Jewellery Quarter'.   I remember that Dad did some out-work for our landlord (who owned a business, also in the Jewellery Quarter) in the evenings to make extra cash.   We never went hungry, were always well dressed and well cared for.   Dad had a good job, and was in fact highly skilled, being an expert in quality control.   He worked for Joseph Lucas from before the war, right up until his retirement in the early '70s.

Dad always made sure that we had a two-week holiday by the sea.   We never stayed in a hotel of course, but would stay in a good quality boarding house on full board.   I would always get excited on the Saturday morning at the start of the holiday, when the black cab would arrive early in the morning to take us to Snow Hill Station and on to the steam train. He did his best for us, and you'd never find him propping up the bar in some pub, unlike many of his contemporaries. He never once raised his hand to me. I have no reason to complain about my childhood. They made mistakes like all parents do, especially my mother, as I think she now realises to her regret. On the whole, they didn't do too badly – after all, hindsight is a wonderful thing.

There's one holiday that's particularly important for two reasons. Dad had rented a converted railway carriage in Yorkshire, and for me as a seven-year-old boy it was a huge adventure. The carriage was parked in the sidings of a country station, and it was during that holiday that I was sexually assaulted. The stationmaster was a man called Scott. One day he lured me into an old barn on the pretext of looking at some wild birds. He put his arm under my chin and lifted up my head, all the time whispering soothing noises in my ear. I became very scared as he put his hand up my shorts, and fondled my private parts. How long this went on for, I don't know, but to me it seemed like forever. When he'd finally got his satisfaction he let me go, and I ran away, frightened out of my life. I've never told anyone that story, and it's recorded here for the first time. As for Scott, let God be his judge.

The second reason that that holiday is important is altogether more pleasurable. There was a young man working at the station, and I can see him in my mind's eye now. About eighteen, short and stocky with a mop of red hair and freckles, he was so handsome that I fell instantly in love with him, and followed him around like a lovelorn puppy. I would take great delight in just sitting and watching him as he worked, stripped to the waist, admiring his sun burned body and rippling muscles. I remember being fascinated by his muscular buttocks, and how excited I got just by looking at him. It's my first real memory of homo-erotic feelings, and one that will stay with me forever. I didn't understand it at the time of course, but realise now that it was an indicator of which direction my sexual orientation would finally lead me. Anyone who wants to play amateur psychiatrist, and link the Scott incident with my homosexuality, would, in my opinion, be totally wrong. Perhaps I should elaborate a little. Human beings are extraordinarily complicated creatures. I feel that to try to relate the incident with Scott to my sexuality would be simplistic in the extreme and inaccurate. I remember talking to a psychiatrist who worked with us on the Friend team in the 1970s. I asked him what made 'A' homosexual and 'B' heterosexual. He smiled, and said, "Dave, if you were to put ten psychiatrists into a room and ask them that question, you'd be given ten different answers." I think that that sums it up.

I sat my eleven-plus exam and failed miserably. Secondary school beckoned, but where was it to be? Gower Street was out as it was reckoned to be one of the toughest schools in Birmingham, full of thugs and delinquents. At least that's what my mother thought. It was decided that Birchfield Road School was the best option, as if all of the boys who went there were little angels. I can't say that my secondary schooldays were in any way happy. During this period of adolescence my private demons were beginning to show themselves for the first time. I struggled with mathematics, and was caned at least once for cheating in an arithmetic exam. Corporal punishment was common in those days, and it wasn't unheard of to get a clip around the ear from those set above us. I remember being slapped across the face by our music teacher during my first year, just before the Christmas concert and bursting into tears. On the way home, Mom and Dad looked at my tear stained face but said nothing.

It was at this time that I lost a huge amount of weight and became as thin as a matchstick. I started to suffer from alopecia, and had a small bald patch at the back of my head. I wouldn't sleep without a light on in the bedroom at night, just like a frightened little boy. Dad even installed an electric bell so that I could summon him in the night. Mom and Dad were so worried that I was sent to see a specialist at the hospital. I clearly remember that he asked me if anything was worrying me at school, and I said no, too frightened to tell him about my fear of the maths class. My self-esteem suffered, not helped by having my successful brother forever pushed into my face.

There is a large age gap between all of the Spencer children. My brother, John, was born in 1937, followed by my sister, Christine, in 1944, and then I appeared in 1948. The youngest, Rosina, seems to have been an after-thought, and came along in 1956. She was the apple of Dad's eye and he doted on her. To put it into some kind of perspective, by the time that I was ten years old, John was already an adult and leading his own life; Christine married whilst I was still at school, and she eventually moved to Australia, where she still lives to this day, and almost entirely disappeared from my life whilst I was still in my teens; when I left home to join the army, Rosina was still a child. So in many ways we were fragmented as children.

I've only ever had two fights in my life, and both of them were at about this time. A fat boy in class decided to bully me (why are they always fat?). It was the biggest mistake of his life. All of my pent up anger came to the surface and I gave him a good hiding, and the ferocity of my attack shocked his little clique so much that they never came near me again. To put it bluntly, I was a mess.

I look back with huge amusement at what was for me the triumph of my secondary school days. My music teacher spotted my talent as a boy soprano. He was a bald little man called Lenny Lowe, who was reputed to play at the *Aston Hippodrome* for the striptease acts in the evenings, and the one that smacked me across the face. He was planning to do Gilbert and Sullivan's comic opera, *HMS Pinafore*, at

Christmas, and I was perfect for the lead female role of Josephine. It wasn't at all unusual for all boy schools to put on operas like this at that time, casting young boy sopranos in the female roles. Josephine has some lovely arias in that opera, but they are very demanding, and require an extremely high range. I sang that part with ease and brought the house down. It was a triumph! By the next year my voice had broken, and I took the male lead in *The Pirates of Penzance*, which was a great success, but I could never surmount my conquest of the previous year. My school days are forever marked in my mind by that performance.

I knocked around with a group from the church. Tony Jefferson and Tommy Leask were two of the lads, while Yvonne Farmer and Carol Bird were some of the girls in the group. We'd spend time together listening to the *Beatles*, and once we all queued up outside the cinema for hours to see Cliff Richard in *Summer Holiday*. Tony's older brother was a Gilbert and Sullivan nut and had every one of the operas on record. Very often after church, we would all come down to No 136, sit in the front room, and listen to one of the operas, drinking coffee. When the *D'Oyly Carte* opera came to Birmingham and played at the *Alexandra Theatre*, we'd get tickets and sit up in the 'Gods'. I loved G & S, as we called it, and still do.

During the bitter winter of 1963, we went down to Carol Bird's house in Guest Street, one evening after church. It was just after Christmas, and the house was well stocked with booze. It stared at us invitingly, and we couldn't resist – I got smashed. I remember Tony helping me through the ice and snow and dumping me at our back gate. He beat a hasty retreat, and I staggered into the living room, looked around and collapsed. Violet was summoned from No 150. She took one look at me and said, 'He's drunk'. She was an expert, having had years of experience with George. It all blew over, as these things do, and was put down to juvenile misbehaviour. I'd had my first taste of the demon drink. It wouldn't be the last, by any means.

The boys that I went to school with were no different from any other boys, and as we matured their eyes strayed towards the opposite sex, while my eyes strayed towards them. I quickly became aware that I found many of them much more interesting than any mere girl, and to my delight discovered that some of them had the same thoughts as me. I remember on a number of occasions having secret trysts with a couple of them after school. It never amounted to much more than a brief and feverish ejaculation, and was really quite innocent. On one occasion after one of these encounters, my partner announced solemnly that from now on he was going after girls, and that would be his last time. Schoolboys are famous for having a crush on other boys and so you shouldn't read too much into it – a quick grope behind the bicycle shed doesn't amount to very much. However, I was certainly sexually active in those days, and the shed at the bottom of our garden was put to good use. I don't know if my reputation followed me around the school, but it's amazing the number of boys who approached me, with only one thing on their minds! Interestingly enough, I don't remember having any great feelings of guilt in those early days – that was to come later. People often say, "Oh, he's just going through a phase." For me, the 'phase' was about to last for the next twelve years of my life.

I knew that I was different, an outsider. Deep down I was aware that this was no mere phase, my homosexuality was very real, and wasn't about to go away. I felt totally isolated and alone. As I write this in 2003, there exists a huge network of gay groups and organisations, ready and willing to offer help to any young gay person who has problems with their sexual identity. For my generation, no such support existed. I quickly became full of self-hate, and turned to the bottle for comfort, not realising that we are unable to escape our inner-selves. The sexual encounters that I was to have in

40

the years that followed were furtive, transient, and riddled with guilt. This was the situation that I found myself in as a 15-year-old boy. I was a victim of my times, and there was nothing that I could do about it. In short, I was a queer!

I turned to drink as a kind of shield or defence mechanism at an early age. Trying to hide inside a bottle doesn't ever work, but many people fool themselves that it does. It's not an unusual phenomenon at all – people drink to excess for a variety of reasons. In my case, I was totally unable to come to terms with my sexuality and used alcohol as a means of hiding from myself. Had I been born twenty or thirty years later, perhaps things would have been different. As it is, I was a victim of my times and, at that time, certainly was not a happy homosexual.

The whole subject of homosexuality in those days was a taboo. Homosexuality was a criminal offence and the police were ruthless with anyone they caught. It was commonplace for gay men to look for other men in public toilets, and the police knew it. They were ever-vigilant, and waited to pounce on the unsuspecting or unwary. The term that comes to mind is 'witch-hunt'. The so-called crime was known as 'soliciting for sex in public places'. The result was a criminal conviction and public shame. Men were forced to live a lie, leading to both guilt and depression and the ever-present fear of discovery. Many took the route of marriage, a smokescreen to hide their true orientation, bringing even more misery to themselves and their families. Only a few short years before, the Nazis had practised a vile persecution of gay men in the concentration camps, something very often conveniently forgotten by many. Britain's treatment of gay men was little better. God only knows the number of homosexuals who killed themselves in despair during the years following the Second World War, but it must have been many. They were made to feel both dirty and furtive by an intolerant society who labelled them 'Queers', 'Poofs' and 'Nancy Boys', something less than men. The 1950s were truly the dark ages for homosexuals. Britain has nothing to be proud of for its treatment of men whose only crime was to be different from the norm.

In 1963 this is what I had to look forward to. For the next twelve years I would be forced to live a lie, to go through the whole gamut of fear, self-loathing and despair. The whole experience has left me extremely angry. Like thousands of gay men before me, my life was almost totally destroyed. Thanks to God, I eventually managed to fight my way through, and come out on the other side. But there was a very heavy price to pay.

It wasn't until the decriminalisation of homosexuality in 1967 that gay men could at last be allowed to be themselves without the fear of prosecution. There was some light at the end of the tunnel, not much, but some. For the armed forces, that freedom was not to be allowed until January of 2000.

I left my schooldays behind me at Easter 1963 without any regret. I didn't have one single qualification, and wondered just what to do with the rest of my life.

Another Volunteer

I enlisted in the British Army as a 'Boy Soldier' on 29ᵗʰ of July 1963, just like my Grandfather Walter before me – although admittedly the circumstances were very different and the country was not at war. I chose The Royal Warwickshire Fusiliers, successor to The Royal Warwickshire Regiment, the county regiment, and part of The Fusilier Brigade. I swore my oath and took the 'Queen's Shilling' at the army recruiting office in Great Charles Street. They had me for nine years, starting on my 18ᵗʰ birthday. As I was only 15, that gave them the first three years for free, not a bad deal, I'd say. Why the army? A good question. It would be easy for me to come up with some deep psychological reason, like running away, a means of escape? Perhaps I was running away, I just don't know. The thought of spending the rest of my life working on some factory floor didn't appeal to me. So fate took a hand, my future was decided, and I joined one of the most homophobic institutions on earth.

Dad delivered me to the Fusilier Brigade Depot at Sutton Coldfield one day in September 1963. I was in, and there was no turning back; my life changed that day. There were about 300 junior soldiers at Sutton – in many ways it was like going to an exclusive boarding school, but with a difference. Although we were only young, the oldest boys being about 18, we were first and foremost soldiers and treated as such. Discipline was tough, and if you were told to jump you jumped, and no questions. The first few days were spent settling in and being issued with a mountain of kit. The boys came from all over the country, Lancashire, Northumberland,

London and of course Warwickshire, and were from similar backgrounds. Our barrack rooms were modern and comfortable, designed for 16 boys and split into four quarters. We soon got into the routine of 'Spit and Polish' – you could see your face in the barrack room floor and the toes of our boots.

There's one boy who sticks in my mind. I'm only mentioning this because it's important to give you some idea of the way people thought then. To put it mildly, he was what is now called 'camp' – he was from London and we called him 'Fancy'. It never occurred to any of us that he was gay, as the whole concept of homosexuality was alien to most of those boys and no one was ever nasty or unpleasant to him. However, the army soon realised their mistake, and he left very soon after joining us. My point is that I was as gay as Fancy, but because my sexuality wasn't obvious, I was able to get away with it. The same fate would have befallen me had the powers that be had any inkling of my sexual preferences.

There's a misconception amongst many people of the stereotype homosexual as being camp and effeminate, but the vast majority of gay men don't fall into that category. During my service I came across men who I now know were gay. The army were also aware that there were gay men in their ranks. I believe they had a good idea who they were, but preferred to turn a blind eye, as long as they were discreet – but God help them if they stepped out of line.

Think about it for a moment. Wherever you have a large society of people, then a certain percentage of them will inevitably be homosexual, that's the way of things. I now believe that homosexuality was more widespread in the armed forces than was ever thought, but by its nature it had to be deeply hidden underground. From time to time throughout my career the army would be rocked by a homosexual scandal of one sort or another – it wasn't that uncommon. As for me, in those days I didn't think of myself as being gay – going through a 'phase' was how I looked at it at the time. I now know of course that I was in denial, but that's not at all unusual.

I learned very early on that the widespread idea that somehow a person can be turned gay is a complete myth. Take it from me, you can't. I also learned very quickly that as far as my new comrades were concerned, you could discreetly look, but you touched at your extreme peril. I wasn't obsessed by my sexuality during every waking hour, but it was always there, lurking just below the surface.

Before I drop this subject and get back to soldiering, there's a story that I'd like to tell. When homosexuality in the armed forces was decriminalised in 2000, there was a great debate in the newspapers. I read an article by a very high-ranking officer who said that two of the bravest and most courageous men that he'd ever served with were gay. He was, however, against the decriminalisation of homosexuality in the forces, which didn't come as a great surprise to me.

A New Beginning
'Oh what a tangled web we weave, when first we practise to deceive.'

One morning a few days after our arrival, a band corporal came into our barrack room carrying a list of names. He was tall and slim, with a large hooked nose, wearing the distinctive yellow hackle of the Lancashire Fusiliers in his beret. Calling us together, he started to read out the names on the list, and mine was one of them. "Right, follow me," he said, after he'd finished, and we all trooped out of the block like so many children being led by the Pied Piper.

We came to a long single-storey building situated next to the Sergeants' Mess and entered a large practice room. We were lined up, told to keep quiet and wait, as the corporal disappeared into a back room. I looked around curiously. Over in one corner sat two young musicians in front of a black metal music stand. They were cornet players, and were playing a duet together. Their bodies swayed gently to the tempo of the music, the notes sounding bell-like as they floated through the air. A little further along sat a short and rather fat clarinet player, who was having great problems with a semi-quaver passage, much to the annoyance of his instructor who growled, "Not like that. Play it again, you wanker." The poor clarinettist started again without much success, but was saved by the entrance of a short, squat man wearing the crown and three stripes of a staff sergeant.

The man shouted in a strong cockney accent, "All right you lot, pack up now and get off to education." He looked at us, squinted, and waddled, rather than walked, over towards the door at the far end of the room. This, I was later to discover, was the instrument store, and the place where the instructors used to hide and drink coffee. The staff sergeant in question was called Jed Watson, a trombonist from the Royal Fusiliers and our boss, on all matters of discipline, for the next two years. From time to time, a door would open and close, as each boy was called in. Eventually it was my turn, and I stood in front of a grey door with a wooden plaque on which was engraved in gold lettering, WO1 [Warrant Officer 1st Class] (BM) Blaber ARCM. I stood and waited, my heart beating and wondering what a WO1 and BM were – I was soon to find out. Another band sergeant, whom I later discovered was called Hebdon, ushered me into a rather small room.

Sitting behind a desk was a diminutive man with red, wavy hair and a thin moustache. He looked up and smiled, not unkindly, telling me to sit down. I studied him as he looked through some papers on his desk. On his left sleeve he wore the Queen's coat of arms, while just above it was a band lyre, signifying that he was a warrant officer first class and bandmaster. Above his left breast pocket was a multicoloured row of medal ribbons, and I didn't need to be told that this man had seen a great deal of service. After a few minutes, Mr Blaber glanced over and asked me to tell him something about myself. I was savvy enough to know that it might be a good idea on my part to tell him how much I liked music, which was true. I was beginning to get the idea what this interview was all about. He smiled and nodded from time to time, finally asking me if I'd like to become a musician. Of course I jumped at the chance, and readily agreed. He looked at me quizzically, saying that I had the mouth of a clarinet player, and that the band of The Royal Warwickshire Fusiliers would soon urgently need clarinet players.

"Very well, Spencer," he said, "You'll be told what to do later by one of the instructors. Send the next one in on your way out." I stood, thanked him and walked out, not realising then that my army career had been mapped out for me in the space of a few minutes of conversation. Not for me the inhospitable plains of northern Germany on a cold winter's night carrying a rifle and pack. Instead, the comfort of the concert hall or bandstand beckoned.

Over the next few months I settled into a routine designed to keep us busy. We all soon became smart and soldierly, marching everywhere around the barracks, while all the time keeping a wary eye out for the much feared Regimental Sergeant Major. The army was well aware of the problem of homesickness in their young charges, and did everything that they could to avoid it. As I said earlier, it was rather like being in a minor public school. Our day consisted of education, music, in the band's case, and sport.

Another lad and myself had a scare with our education. The army insisted that all of its recruits passed the third class army education examination. This certificate would enable us to reach the rank of sergeant. My old friend, arithmetic, nearly caused my downfall, but I managed to scrape through on the third and last attempt with, I suspect, a little help from the education officers.

I soon got used to the clarinet and discovered a love of playing. The army knew that they had two-and-a-half years to train us as musicians, and in a measured way slowly but surely they bought out the best in us. It was a system that worked well. None of us were ever going to be great musicians and play principal clarinet with *The London Symphony Orchestra*, for example, but they wanted good solid players and generally succeeded. With so much time available, you can learn an awful lot. We started on the musical equivalent of the 'Janet and John' early reading books, called 'A tune a day', and progressed on to more difficult tutors. We all soon became pretty efficient and looked forward eagerly to the day when we would be allowed to sit down in the full band. Our instructors were a good bunch, all of whom were on a two year tour from their bands, and we learned a lot from them.

The other boys and myself soon discovered the joy to be had playing beautiful music with other musicians, something that I've carried with me my whole life. Like just about everything else in the army, the whole system has changed now. Today they have an Army Corps of Music, and to be accepted you have to have a high standard of musicianship before they'll take you.

The army and bullshit are very good friends. We quickly learned the art of 'Spit and Polish', and our boots gleamed. For the first time in my life I picked up an iron and learned how to use it. We were transformed from a bunch of snotty nosed kids into smart, well turned out young men – an old fashioned concept now. Our accommodation gleamed. We spent a huge amount of our time preparing for one inspection or another, and were forever complaining – in short, we learned discipline.

The Company Commander's inspection on Saturday morning was the one that we dreaded. We would be standing by our beds as he did his rounds, glancing nervously towards the door as he approached ever nearer. At last we were called to attention and stood rigidly as he prowled around, looking in the most unlikely places for dust. We all breathed a sigh of relief as he nodded and walked out satisfied, wishing us all a good weekend.

At 6.00 o'clock each morning our barrack room would echo with the cry, "Hands off cocks and on with your socks," as the duty NCO burst in – God help you if you were still in bed a few minutes later when he returned. After breakfast, we would spend time scrubbing and polishing the ablutions and our rooms, after stripping our beds and folding the sheets and blankets, making what we called 'bed boxes'.

The Band of the Junior Soldiers Company
Sutton Coldfield about 1964

Following that we had muster parade. We fell in for inspection in three ranks, and were expected to be immaculately dressed. The transformation in a few short months was incredible. I grew in stature and confidence. No one who knew me would have recognised me. We were very quickly learning the meaning of personal pride and were taught to have pride in our regiments and ourselves.

I soon discovered that I had a natural talent for long-distance running and was never happier than when I returned from a long run absolutely covered in mud. I was as thin as a stick – there was, as they say, "More fat on a butcher's pencil." For a long time there was one boy I could never beat, and a friendly rivalry sprang up between us. It wasn't long before I set myself the goal of beating him at all costs, and I was ruthless in my determination. He was like a whippet, but one day I managed to get into the lead and stay there. First I came abreast of him, and then slowly drew ahead, as a look of dismay flashed over his face. He was totally deflated, and never beat me again after that.

My greatest triumph was to take the third prize in the Western Command championships, competing against some of the best long-distance runners in the army. I'm not trying to crow about my achievements, but merely to illustrate the change that had transformed me from a boy who had had no confidence in his abilities, to someone who had.

I was never any good at athletics. Even the mile was too short a distance for me. I preferred the long, hard slog. The officer in charge, a young lieutenant called Rennick, insisted that I run the mile. I was given no choice, and certainly couldn't refuse. The event was an inter-army athletics meeting and the competition was fierce. We started off and I soon trailed behind. On the last lap my running shoe came loose and fell off. Unfortunately, a strap attached it to my ankle and I couldn't get rid of it. I had two options, either stop or carry on. As I was already last, I was determined not to make myself look more of a fool than I already felt, and so continued, much to the delight of the crowd. A huge roar of appreciation erupted all around the stadium as I limped in. It was a bloody stupid thing to do, the spikes on those shoes were extremely sharp and I could have badly injured myself, but my determination overcame my common sense. Childish, but I couldn't help myself. I was promoted to Junior Lance Corporal just after that.

I don't know how it all came about, but there was another boy in my intake, a flute player, who I'll call Ken (names of people I have had a relationship with in those days have been changed). Ken had light brown wavy hair, blue eyes, and was a little on the plump side, which somehow added to the attraction. We quickly realised that we were both on the same wavelength sexually – I'd found an ally.

Ken approached me one day, making sure that no one else was within earshot, and quietly suggested that I join him in the camp library that evening. I agreed eagerly, as he suggested that we both wear our tracksuits. I knew exactly what was going through his mind, and spent the rest of the day in anticipation.

The camp library was situated in the education block and was quite isolated. Ken or myself would go to the guardroom and sign for the key, and later we would meet up separately. We were always careful not to be seen together too often. It was rare for anyone to bother to take books out in the evenings, and so we usually had the place to ourselves. We made sure that we wore our tracksuits with little else underneath – most boys wore tracksuits in the evenings, and so no one noticed or thought it unusual. From time to time, we'd look at each other across the table, and smile, both aware of our sexual arousal. After a decent interval of excited anticipation, we would lock the front door to the building, giving us total privacy. The toilets in the building were windowless, and that's where we retired and spent half an hour of uninhibited sexual pleasure.

Another favourite for us was the band block. On the excuse of doing extra practice, we'd go across in the evenings and the same procedure would follow. Ken and I had this relationship for most of our boys' service. We were playing a very dangerous game, but this only added to the excitement. To the best of my knowledge, no one ever suspected a thing, or at least if they did, they never said anything. I remember that we nearly got caught out on one occasion. We were in the band practice rooms with the door locked when we heard it violently rattle. Quickly rearranging ourselves, Ken went to answer it. Standing there was one of the other junior bandsmen who had come across from the weekly dance. The record player had broken and they needed to use the band's player that was, of course, kept in the band block. I remember that he gave us both a puzzled look as he walked out.

The weekly dance was an eagerly anticipated event amongst the boys. The local girls were invited and came in droves, and I'm sure that many of those lads and lasses lost their virginity on those nights of romance behind the NAAFI. Needless to say, neither Ken nor myself ever attended one. I often wonder if any eyebrows were ever raised.

Our affair only ended when we went our separate ways and to different bands. This arrangement would have been idyllic, but for one thing – guilt. I always felt guilty. I was a product of my environment and my society. This guilt about my homosexuality was to stay with me for many years and would be devastating. For many gay men of my generation, this was to prove a great problem. We'd been brought up to regard homosexuality as an abomination by the society that we lived in. Is it any wonder therefore that many of us regarded ourselves with self-loathing?

I found what I thought was a solution – of course it wasn't, it was an attempt at escape and, as I've already said, we can't escape our inner-selves no matter how hard we try. Alcohol was forbidden to us boys, as we were all underage at the time. Living so close to the barracks, I was able to go home for a few hours at the weekends. I've often regretted being so close to home in those days – it would have been better for me to be miles away. Anyway, I would often travel home, and then go to the off-licence and buy cider. I would sit in the front room and get quietly drunk. Not so bad that you would notice, but I'd drink enough so that my sense of guilt would disappear for a while, giving me a false feeling of well being – until the next time, and there always was a next time.

Ironically, there was only one time during my service that I got into trouble because of drink, and that was on boys' service. I'd been out and had more than usual. I managed to get past the beady eye of the duty NCO, but as I lay in bed, the ceiling started to spin, and before I could jump out I vomited all over the floor. The next morning the duty NCO came in to wake me up and saw the mess on the floor – I was charged. The Company Commander said that if I wanted to act like a man, then he would treat me like one, and fined me £10, a huge amount in those days.

I remember taking a boy called Peter home with me one Sunday evening. I knew that my parents would be going to church that night, leaving the field free. I proceeded to get Peter drunk with the hope that I could seduce him. Unfortunately he wasn't having it and we returned to barracks. Even in those early days, I was beginning to take very dangerous risks. In later years Peter and I went on to serve together in the same band and became very close friends, a friendship that's lasted until this day. As far as I know, he never said anything to anyone about that night.

Both Ken and Peter served in the army for 22 years, reaching the rank of Staff Sergeant, but they never liked each other. It's also interesting to note that Ken later married and had a daughter, although sadly his wife died of cancer. So was he gay? Yes, I think that he was. Like many gay men of our generation, he chose to take the marriage route as a way of hiding his true orientation.

There's an interesting post-script to the story of Peter. Many years after leaving the army I tracked him down, one of the first of many. I wrote to him, received a reply, and wrote back again giving him my history. I told him everything that had happened to me in the intervening years since our last meeting. By that time, I was long out of the closet and leading a happy life with Martin. So I was both puzzled and angry when I received no reply. After all, he'd known that I was gay from the beginning. I wrote him a stinking letter, threw his address in the bin and forgot about him.

Some years later, at about 1.00 am, we were in bed asleep when the phone rang. I got up and answered it. On the other end of the line was Peter's wife, Kay – I was amazed. She went on to tell me that when my letter had arrived their son, Darren, had just come out as gay. He was 19, and Peter was having great problems in accepting his son's homosexuality, something I understood perfectly because I had seen it happen so many times before. I persuaded Kay to get Peter to ring me, which he did. Since then we've become good friends and visit each other from time to time. Darren is now a successful young man of 25, and doing very well for himself.

Every time that I think of the following incident I chuckle with amusement at the irony of it all. Martin and I spent a weekend with Peter and Kay. Peter suggested that it would be better if Martin and I stayed with Darren and his lover, Phillip, as they had more room. We readily agreed. Phillip, a stocky, blond-haired lad in his early twenties, thought that it would be a good idea for the four of us to visit a large gay club in Coventry. I was more than a bit dubious, as I was in my mid-fifties and thought my clubbing days long over. But Martin was up for it, and so it was decided that Peter would run the four of us over in the car, and later we would take a taxi back home. On our way there I had a mental picture of myself trying to get the beautiful Peter drunk and then seduce him – and here we were, over thirty years later, being driven to a gay club by the self same Peter and his gay son and lover. I couldn't control myself and started to crack up with laughter. Peter turned to me, a look of puzzlement across his face. Before he could say anything, I lifted my hand and said, "Don't ask, Peter, please don't ask!"

The four of us had a wonderful evening. I couldn't help but study these handsome young men, both so at ease with themselves and their sexuality, comparing them with myself and the mess that I had been in at the same age. Darren, tall, dark and handsome, just as his father had been, was laughing and at ease as he teased Phillip. I envied them as I reflected how times had changed, and couldn't help but feel just a little bit bitter. I looked around at these young gay men and women, seemingly without a care in the world, having a great Saturday night out. I wondered how my life would have turned out had I had the opportunity to live my life like them at the same age. Mentally I admonished myself and looked towards Martin. We smiled at each other, our love as strong as it had ever been, as I reminded myself that I should count my blessings and stop feeling sorry for myself. The four of us rolled home in the early hours of the morning, tired but happy.

Towards the end of my boys' service, we had a big open day at the barracks and all of the parents were invited. My conducting talent had soon been noticed and encouraged. Blaber had left the army early in my career and had been replaced by a bandmaster called Kimberley. He was to go on to reach the highest echelons in army music. I remember an incident one day in full band, when Kimberly was conducting. He looked down at me and stopped the band. "Spencer," he said, "you're supposed to be a musician, not a gardener." I didn't understand until he pointed to my fingernails. They were filthy.

As the open day approached Kimberly amazed me by handing me his baton, saying, "Conduct this Spencer." I stood in front of the band and with great confidence conducted the piece from beginning to end. When I had finished he nodded and said, "Good, I want you to conduct that at the open day concert." You can imagine my pride that day. Dad must have been watching me with his mind going back all of those years to my childhood and 'Friday Night Is Music Night'. After the concert, a lad called Philip Sowden came over to speak to me. I was surprised as he and I never

got on. Perhaps he had sensed my eyes looking at him a little too intensely. He was an infantryman, tall, slim, and very macho with no particular interest in music. I, on the other hand, had a great deal of interest in him. I was amazed when he held out his hand and shook mine, saying, "Well done Spencer, that was bloody good." I smiled and thanked him. I've often wondered what happened to him.

I won the best all-round musician prize that year. I remember that my heart was singing that day, as I got changed ready to go home on a long summer leave. As I got into the car, Dad looked at me and beamed with pride as he drove off. My boys' service days came to an end just after that summer. The two years seemed to have passed in a flash. I was seventeen-and-a-half, and the army, in their wisdom, decreed that I was now a man. It was time to move on to the next stage of my army career. I wondered what the future held for me.

The Twilight Years

On 22nd of October 1965 I flew out of Britain to join my regiment in Hamlin, of 'Pied Piper' fame. I'll never forget my feelings of excitement, mixed with a little fear of the unknown. Out of necessity the army were obliged to keep us boys on a tight rein, but I'd heard the stories of the freedoms available to a young soldier after the straight-jacket of boys' service, and I wanted some of it.

The plane touched down on a cold, grey evening. After we had collected our kit and exited the airport, a long line of three-ton army lorries and their drivers greeted us. A young but hard-bitten NCO told us to throw our things in to the back of the lorries, get aboard and to be quick about it. He looked us up and down with contempt, as if saying, "Your days of playing at soldiers are over, this is the real thing, and you'd better get used to it quickly." As the transport pulled away, we huddled together for mutual support and looked at the strange and foreign town as it passed us by. For many this was their first time away from England and home. The convoy drove into the barrack gates and on to the parade square. Almost as soon as they'd come to a halt, the drivers jumped from their cabs and lowered the tailgates, ordering us to get down. We obeyed and stood looking around us at this strange, new world.

A group of soldiers were visible in the dark walking alongside the square, carrying knives, forks, spoons and enormous mugs, heading towards the illuminated windows of the cookhouse. They looked across as one of them said something, and they all laughed. One wag shouted over, "You'll fucking regret it, you wankers," while another gave the accompanying hand gesture. I shivered. They were like alien beings – gone was my new found feeling of freedom, to be replaced by a very real fear of the unknown. At that moment a sergeant and two corporals came into sight. They stopped and stared at us. The sergeant was a large man with the face of the heavyweight boxer that he was, together with a look in his eye which spoke volumes. "Get fell in and answer your names," he growled. As we fell over ourselves to obey, the two corporals walked around us like sheep dogs, keeping a wary eye on their charges. After the roll call we were marched off the square and over to a three-storied barrack block. Above the wide entrance I was amazed to see an eagle etched in stone, the swastika that once stood underneath long since obliterated. These barracks had been standing since the time of Bismarck, and had housed armies ever since. The eagle stood as a stark reminder of recent history.

The two corporals by now were showing the new intake to their barrack rooms. Feeling like Oliver Twist, I nervously approached the sergeant and timidly said, "Excuse me Sergeant, but I'm for the band." He looked me over. "What's your name, son?" he asked with a glint in his eye. I told him. He muttered something and walked away. A few minutes later he returned, and to my great relief, said, "Wait there. Someone will be over to pick you up." I'd had visions that it was all a big mistake and that I was not going to be in the band after all. The prospect of those cold, German plains filled me with dread.

At last a familiar face appeared. Dave Panton had been on boys' service with me; being older he'd left the previous year to join the regiment. We'd been very good friends, and as he approached he smiled and held out his hand, saying, "Hello, Dave, welcome. Come on, let's get out of here. There's too many squaddies around for me." He stooped, picked up my kit-bag and headed out into the night, and I followed closely behind. He led me into a room with a polished wooden floor and four large, grey lockers and beds. Each bed space was adorned with multicoloured posters, giving it a homely feel. There was a space in one corner with an empty bed and locker, which I assumed was mine. This was real luxury after the sixteen-man rooms that I'd been used to. We went down to the store and I drew out some bedding before heading towards the cookhouse and a tea of sausage, egg and chips. I was starving and devoured it with relish.

Dave was an oboe player and would-be composer. I got the distinct impression that his view of the army was beginning to sour. On boys' service he'd always sported a regimental blazer and carried an umbrella. That was all to change radically in the not too far distant future. After we returned to the barracks, I was puzzled to see the place so empty and asked him where the other members of the band were. He told me that they were all on leave and wouldn't be back for a few days. He sat with me talking over old times as I unpacked. "Where are your civvies?" he suddenly asked. A look of horror crossed his face as I explained that we'd been forbidden to pack any, and that they were all in my MFO box and would follow on later. "You prat!" he said. "Do you mean that you've no civilian clothes at all?" Sheepishly I nodded my head, as he continued, "Well, if you think that I'm going out of these barracks with you dressed in uniform, you're mistaken. You can borrow something of mine for now." I nodded gratefully. When I'd packed, I'd been thinking like a boy soldier. The order was no civilian clothes, and so it was no civilian clothes. I'd learned my first lesson. Stop thinking like a robot and start thinking for myself. As I look back on those days all these years later, I realise just how much the army had programmed us boys into being little automatons.

Sometime later I ventured out alone into the camp in search of the NAAFI. First I went to the shop to buy toothpaste and polish. As I came downstairs, just to my right were two swing doors. Making up my mind, I pushed them open and entered a large, well-stocked bar. The room was blue with a fog of cigarette smoke, the babble of voices filling the air. Most of the tables were occupied, their surfaces covered with empty bottles and overflowing ashtrays. The men sitting around the tables were dressed in a variety of clothes, some in T-shirts and jeans, others in uniform, as they talked animatedly amongst themselves. The duty corporal poked his head around the door, glanced in, and satisfied, headed back in the direction of the corporal's mess. He knew that it was still too early for the trouble that often flared up over some imagined slight or other.

Walking over to the bar I waited while two tattooed squaddies ordered their beers and sauntered away, taking no notice of me. The barman turned to me and smiled. I'd noticed him as I'd waited, my interest aroused. He was small, with black, curly hair and obviously gay. I was amazed. Here we were, surrounded by these butch, macho men, and this man was totally unaffected by his surroundings or the men around him. I later learned that he was held in some affection by the soldiers, a bit like a queer mascot. I've often wondered if he ever scored. "What can I get you?" he said, looking me up and down keenly, a smile playing at the corner of his mouth. "Christ," I remember thinking to myself, "does he know?" I hesitated and said, nervously, "A beer, please."

"Right you are then," he said, camply, placing a bottle of *Amstel* on the counter and taking my money. He turned away, as I surreptitiously eyed his backside, before cursing myself for an idiot and coming sharply back to reality. He was now serving another customer, and totally oblivious to me, as I walked away and found an empty table. I took my first legal sip of beer and sighed with contentment as I lit a cigarette and looked around. That room was every gay man's idea of heaven, full of beautiful, muscular young men and the fact that they were forbidden made it all the more exciting. Two hours and several bottles of beer later, I stood up and walked out. A buzz rushed through my body as I strolled back to the barracks. I'd had my first fix and it felt great, the genie was out of the bottle, and it would be a very long time before it went back in again.

The next morning, I was sitting on the edge of my bed when Dave walked in. "The BM wants to see you. Come on, I'll show you," he said leading me out of the room. Jim Parkinson was a slightly built man, with greying hair. He looked up as I knocked and walked in.

"Morning, Spencer," he said, shaking my hand, "Take a seat." I sat facing him, as he pushed a packet of cigarettes across the desk towards me, indicating that I should help myself. I was gobsmacked! An army bandmaster, treating me almost as an equal. I said, "Thank you, sir," lit up, and waited.

"Welcome to the band," he said, "I'm bloody glad to have you. We desperately need good clarinet players, and I've heard nice things about you. I want you to get an instrument out of the stores and tomorrow I'll do your trade test. I'm sorry that I couldn't send you down to Kneller Hall (The Royal Military School of Music) but you're young, so we'll see what we can do in a couple of years time."

I nodded and said, "Thank you, sir," excited at the thought of passing my trade test and the extra cash that that would put into my pocket. I went to the instrument store, took out a clarinet, and started to practise.

That evening I went back to the NAFFI and had a few beers. The gay barman had been replaced by a large-breasted peroxide blonde called Betty, who seemed to know everyone, and was referred to by many of the squaddies, disparagingly, as the camp bicycle. As I was sitting there, I overheard a conversation between two young soldiers that went something like this:

1st Soldier: "Have you heard the news?" (excitedly)

2nd Soldier: "No, what news?"

1st Soldier: "There are two queers in 'B' company."

2nd Soldier: "You're fucking joking."

1st Soldier: "I'm not you know," (with relish). Taking a large gulp of beer, he continued, "Apparently, these two poofs went to the company commander this morning and told him that they were queer."

2nd Soldier: "Bollocks!"

1st Soldier: "It's true, I tell you. Anyway, they told him that they were in love with one another."

2nd Soldier: "Well fuck me."

1st Soldier: "No thanks, mate. Two queers in the regiment's enough."

2nd Soldier: "You know what I mean, you wanker. What do you think will happen to the dirty bastards? Do you think that they'll be sent to Colchester?"

1st Soldier: "Fuck knows. If it were left to me, I'd lock them up and throw away the key. Fucking perverts."

2nd Soldier: "Yeh, I hate queers. The thought of it makes me shudder. Come on, drink up, It's your fucking round, and I'll have a whisky to go with it."

The first soldier nodded, got up and headed towards the bar. I watched him go. The lesson of that conversation was not lost on me.

The next morning I nervously entered Parkinson's office, emerging half an hour later, an 'A' class tradesman and military musician, one of the highest trades in the British Army. The members of the band started to return from leave that evening, and I was submerged in a whole new society. I was the new boy, and for a few weeks I wasn't allowed to forget it.

The only other person that I knew from boys' service was a tall, thin trombone player called Harvey Smith. In fact his full name was Harvey Ransom Lloyd Smith – the 'Smith', I always thought, was a bit of a let down. He sported a crew cut and wore black-rimmed spectacles. We'd been together since our first day as boys at Sutton Coldfield and got on well. To put it mildly, the members of the band were the most dreadful snobs, and we regarded ourselves as being far superior to any squaddie. We saw ourselves as the white-collar workers of the regiment and never got our hands dirty on the shop floor. I say 'we', because I quickly became the same. No guard duties for us, and no running around with a rifle on a cold winter's night wearing a full pack in a howling gale. We led a totally separate life, living in a musical world, and only socialising with each other and other musicians. To the other members of the regiment, the band was made up of a load of 'poofs'. Many of the older and more experienced members looked down on me with something akin to disdain. I had to prove myself worthy before being admitted to their exclusive little club. Later, I was to do exactly the same thing with new boys who joined us. One of the most difficult things for me to get used to was rank. Except for the bandmaster and band sergeant, we always called each other by our first names. Having just coming from such a highly disciplined society, where rank was everything, it was very hard for me to get used to for a while. Also, I quickly learned that unlike boys' service, no one was going to run around after me and that I had to look after myself.

One of my roommates was a young man called Paul, and I fancied him like mad. He was from the north of England, unlike most of the others who generally came from the Midlands. Short and stocky, with slicked back hair, he gave an air of confidence which I found attractive. On many mornings I'd lie in bed, and with my eyes half closed, feigning sleep, surreptitiously watching him. He always slept in mini-briefs, and would lie stretched out, one foot dangling over the edge of the bed, the bedclothes pushed down to his knees – something that I found highly erotic. Paul would lie there still half-asleep staring at the ceiling and taking the occasional drag of his first cigarette of the day. Whether or not he guessed that he was being watched and was putting on a show, I'll never know, but I fantasised over him endlessly, leading to great frustration. I was to learn something later that would make me wish that I'd made some kind of approach towards him. The thought of having a sexual liaison with Peter was very attractive. As it was, I had to make do with a hand job.

Our whole day was filled with making music. As I sat down for the first time I began to realise just what good musicians some of these people were. Parkinson put me down on first clarinet, a position that I was to hold for most of my army musical career. I was very proud, as being so young and new, I'd expected to be playing on the third clarinet stand. I can't tell you what a delight it was for me to be playing such challenging music – the pleasure that I got from it was enormous.

We were versatile. The band had a very good dance band led by a sergeant called Bazz. This group was in great demand for various functions and the players made themselves a great deal of money on the side, often keeping very late nights in the process. There was a pop group and a folk music group. Harvey Smith was in both. During our time in Watchet, Harvey, and a lad called Terry, did very well for themselves, playing 'Dubliners' type music in one of the local pubs for holidaymakers. We played church music, something that I really enjoyed, and I would often get together with one of the other clarinet players and play duets. The one duty that none of us liked was passing out parades, but we were in great demand for these occasions. It was usually icy cold, with the wind whistling across the parade square. As it's impossible to play a clarinet wearing gloves, our fingers were so frozen that after a while it was almost agony to play.

The social life of the band revolved around the band club. This phenomenon was universally adopted by just about every military band in the British Army at the time. Usually situated in the attic, it was a place that we used as often as possible. Not for us the NAFFI bar, we were far too superior to be seen using that place, and anyone who did could expect to be frowned upon by the other band members. After all, we were not squaddies, were we?

I'll never forget the first night that I walked into the club. Standing behind the bar was a chap called Maurice, a Brummie with tattoos all over his arms, who everyone called 'Mo'. I ordered an *Amstel*, and told him to have one himself, which cheered him up, as he was a rather dour bloke. That evening I used a bit of common-sense, and as each person came in, brought them a drink, hoping to integrate myself with everyone. Mo was a very good saxophone player, and one of the leading lights in the dance band. He was a great mate of a flute player called Frank, who was as mad as a hatter, and I often saw the two of them pissed out of their minds, serenading each other like medieval troubadours. They were inseparable, like Siamese twins. Legend has it that Maurice bought a set of bagpipes and took them up to the attic to practise. Soon the whole building was filled with the eerie wailing of the pipes, and Frank convinced himself that the place was haunted, something that Maurice encouraged with glee.

I made friends with a little Brummie cornet player called Harry. Harry's only claim to musical fame was his ability to make a 'neighing' sound on his cornet, something that was in great demand at Christmas time when we played Leroy Anderson's 'Sleigh Ride'. Harry wasn't the best musician in the world but he was a good bloke. We'd often go into town, get plastered, and end up in some greasy cafe eating egg and chips. I lost count of the hours that we spent in that bar drinking, and we would often stagger back to our beds in the early hours of the morning. As we were all heavy drinkers, I was able to blend in, something that suited my purposes very well. As Christmas approached during my first winter with the band in 1965 I had begun to be accepted. Harry, myself, and a few others took the train to the Hook of Holland and sailed to England and home for the Christmas leave, getting thoroughly pissed on the way.

Often, on Sunday mornings, I'd get up early and walk over to the 'Red Shield Club' which was run by The Salvation Army. I'd buy two or three Sunday papers and go to a nice little restaurant that I'd discovered. The headwaiter was a tall, distinguished man of about sixty, and always extremely polite. I've often regretted that we didn't share a common language, as it would have been nice to speak to him, and hear his history. I'd sit there for hours, drinking beer and reading the papers. As lunchtime approached, I'd order a steak and devour it with relish. This was my way of escaping barrack room life, something that I never got used to, and always felt uncomfortable with.

At the beginning of 1966 on our return from Christmas leave, the regiment started to make preparations for the move back to the UK. The band had one last duty to perform. Along with the two other regimental bands in the garrison, we were to give a farewell Gala Concert in the plush town concert hall. One of the bands was from a cavalry regiment – I was always jealous of these boys, as their uniforms with gold piping were splendid. They wore extremely tight trousers and spurs. The effect was stunningly sexy, and I often dreamed about one of their clarinet players, all to no avail, unfortunately. In the years that followed I played many splendid concerts, but that one will stay in my memory forever. It was a glittering affair, with over a hundred musicians on the concert platform. Amongst other things, we played the Franz Von Suppé overture to 'Poet and Peasant', a great favourite of my father's. The grand march from Wagner's opera 'Tannhauser' and the ballet suite to Delibes' 'Coppelia' followed. The finalé was the famous Rossini overture, 'William Tell', whose clarinet parts are horrendously difficult. And so I'd had my first taste of army musical life, and loved it. If only my own personal demons would have left me in peace, I would have been content, but for the foreseeable future that just couldn't be.

It's difficult for me to put into words with any clarity my feelings in those days. The confidence that had been fostered and grown inside of me on boys' service quickly disappeared, to be replaced by a permanent nervousness. When I drank, I regained a measure of confidence. The feeling was all pervasive, and never left me from one day to the next. Fortunately I was popular – that helped, and I don't suppose for one minute that the others noticed. On the surface I was my usual cheerful self. Inside, however, I had this feeling that if anyone looked closely enough they would be able to see the real me, the queer. I had to avoid that at all costs. I stopped going to the cookhouse to eat and survived on sandwiches, which didn't do me any good at all. The fear of walking into the place filled me with dread, and so I avoided it. On the one hand I had these strong sexual feelings, which I liked, and on the other I hated myself for them. In the army there is no privacy and no escape from other people. You can't go home at night, shut the door, and be alone. Years later I was able to do something about this problem, when, by finding a place of my own and living away from barracks, I was at last able to find the privacy that I craved. But that was a long time into the future and I had no choice but to live with it.

In recent years I've often been asked why I stayed in and put myself through this torture. The answer is that it would have been the same wherever I was. I was still a product of my society and upbringing, and I doubt that anything would have been much different anywhere else. Also, getting out of the army wasn't that easy. It would have cost me a great deal of money, which I didn't have, and anyway, it's doubtful that they would have let me go. I often think of those days as my 'Spy Days', the time when I had to submerge my true identity and pretend to be something that I wasn't. To sum it all up, my fears and anxieties dominated my entire being, my every waking moment, leaving it very difficult for me to be able to function in a normal way.

To be fair, and to give a balanced picture, I should show the other side of the coin. I got along well with my fellow musicians and was popular. If they did know about me, they said nothing. As a musician I had a wonderful life doing something that I loved. Music was important to me, and my love of music has stayed with me all of my life. In fact I've never stopped playing for any length of time – everything from chamber music, orchestral music and band music.

There's a huge irony in my almost accidental involvement in the professional music business. The Spencer side of the family has always been deeply involved in music, going back to late Victorian times. My grandfather, William, was a fine violinist, and encouraged all of his children to play. My Aunt Alice, who died very young, was reputed to be a gifted pianist and would sit for hours playing. Dad was both a cellist and a pianist. Musical evenings were the norm within the Spencer household, with everyone taking part. Between the two wars, Dad often played with cinema orchestras, during the silent picture era and played with the prestigious YMCA orchestra. His teacher was a well-known Polish cellist, whose name I've now forgotten.

Dad encouraged all of us to learn the piano. My brother and two sisters did this, whereas I showed not the slightest interest and resisted any attempt to get me to play. Dad was wise enough not to try to force me. I get very annoyed with parents who try to force their children to play musical instruments, when it's patently obvious that the child has no real interest. Once I gave a young boy clarinet lessons for a couple of years and he was doing well. However, when I told him that he should start playing within a musical group and he refused, I advised him to put the instrument back into its case and forget about it. Music is a group activity. Anyone who tries to play alone for any length of time will soon get very bored indeed, and will eventually lose interest.

At secondary school, we were forced to play the recorder as a group activity, and I absolutely loathed it. I was terrible and couldn't tell the difference between a crotchet and a quaver. Yet two years later, I was quickly becoming a competent clarinettist. This is one debt that I owe to the army. My love of music began during my boys' service, a love that I carry with me to this day. I can't explain the buzz that you get when you sit with a group of musicians and play a symphony by one of the great composers, or a suite for band by someone like Gustav Holst. I love playing chamber music – the wonderful Mozart clarinet quintet comes to mind. I remember spending a delightful evening playing this sublime music, perhaps one of the finest pieces ever written for the clarinet, and even if I say it myself, I didn't make a bad job of it.

I quickly discovered a gift for conducting and would love to stand in front of the band, conducting an overture or a selection from opera. Just before I left the army, Rod Parker invited me to conduct the band in the Redditch theatre, as I was a local lad. I conducted the overture to 'Light Cavalry'. During my last months at Bassinbourne, before everything came crashing down, I was privileged to be asked to conduct the premier of a work for children's choir and wind band. That performance was without doubt one of the highpoints of my conducting career.

My one great regret is that conducting is something that I never carried on with. Luxembourg is full of wind bands and had I tried, I would have been quickly taken up. The problem was one of language, and I just didn't have the confidence to rehearse a group of musicians in a foreign language. If I'd been living in England, I think that by now I would have led a very active musical life as an amateur conductor. I rather mischievously threw down the gauntlet to my brother recently. He is very involved in amateur operatics and fancies himself as a conductor. I suggested that we might do a joint concert together. The offer was never taken up.

Conducting apart, I've had a wonderful musical life and been privileged to play with some very fine musicians. I am more than content.

Our stay in Watchet, Somerset was to last for three years, from 1966 to 1969, although it seemed much longer than that. Granted, the barracks were sub-standard, but for all that, it was a very nice place to be. The town is set on the coast facing the Bristol Channel, with a small harbour and only one main street. The town made its living from a shirt factory, a paper making plant, and of course, tourists. Minehead was just a few miles further along the coast, and boasted a *Butlin's* holiday camp. The surrounding countryside, framed by the Quantock Hills, is of outstanding beauty, some of the best in England. The barracks were situated about two miles along the coast from Watchet. The two band blocks overlooked the water, and in summer it was idyllic.

One evening I decided to go out alone. About two miles from the camp was the small village of Williton. There were only two pubs in the village – in fact one was a hotel called *The Egremont*. I had a very good reason for going to *The Egremont*, and his name was Patrick. Patrick served in the posh lounge bar, and I was very taken with him. He was always immaculately dressed, and an extremely snobbish young man in his early twenties with a public school accent, which was part of the attraction. I couldn't get enough of him. He was stocky and handsome, with dark hair, and the face of a dirty-minded angel. I ordered my drink and sat down. The only other person in the bar was a well-to-do middle aged farmer, who was having a conversation with Patrick. They were talking quietly, and I listened without being too obvious. Patrick was explaining patiently to the farmer that, yes, he was gay, and didn't have any problem with it. The farmer was horrified, and urged Patrick to see a doctor and get himself cured. "After all," he said, "it's not natural, is it?" Patrick was exasperated, and said, "But it's

72

natural to me, and that's all that matters." All of this time I was listening in, my heart beating rapidly, as they argued quietly back and forth. I was amazed. That was the first time that I'd ever heard a man openly admit that he was gay, and I admired him for it. This would have been about the time of decriminalisation of homosexuality in England. I had a few more drinks and left, a plan beginning to form in my mind.

A few nights later, I went back. I knew that Patrick lived on the premises, and hoped that if I could manage to stay late enough, I might get an invitation. It was a forlorn hope. The bell for last orders had been rung, and I was the only one left. I was chatting to Patrick when the door opened, and a blond-haired young man entered. Patrick was delighted, and I can't say that I blamed him. As they say, 'two's company and three's a crowd', and so I asked Patrick if he'd call me a cab and left, my hopes dashed. Of course he had no way of knowing that I was gay, and even if he had, he may not necessarily have fancied me.

I've often asked this question of heterosexual friends, "Do you find every young woman that you meet sexually attractive?" They usually look at you as if you're mad, and say, "No, of course not." My reply's always the same, "Then why do you think that it's any different for me?" People have this idea that gay men sleep with each other like rabbits, just because they happen to be gay and are together in the same room. Take it from me, it's not true. At least, not in my experience. I'll return to Patrick a little later.

I was on leave and alone. In fact I had the place to myself and was feeling very randy indeed, but what could I do about it? Mom had written me a letter telling me that she and Dad would be away on holiday, and that I'd have to fend for myself. Great, I thought, as I lay soaking in a hot bath playing with my erection and taking long swigs from a bottle of pale ale. A white fog of steam filled the bathroom, as I luxuriated tipsily in the piping hot water, and remembered a boy from my schooldays, who wasn't averse to a bit of sexual fun. Making up my mind, I dried myself off, got dressed and walked down the street to the telephone box. I hurriedly, almost hungrily, leafed through the tattered telephone directory, and prayed that I'd be able to find him. Spotting the name and number, I quickly dialled, my heart beating a tattoo in my chest as I waited impatiently.

Mrs Phillips answered the phone and I politely introduced myself. "Oh, hello, David. Yes, Ronald is here. Just one moment," she said, putting down the receiver with a clank.

"Let him be up for it," I prayed, as I waited, my fingers nervously entwined around the plastic telephone cord.
"Hello," came the familiar voice from the other end of the line, as my mind feverishly replayed the number of times that we'd played together.
"It's Dave Spencer, do you remember me, Ronald?"
He chuckled, as he replied, "Of course. How could I possibly forget you, Dave?" I could see his girlish face, red lips, and slightly plump body, and I felt my own body respond. I quickly explained that I had the place to myself, and would he like to come over for the evening? He didn't hesitate, as he said, "I'd be delighted."
Emboldened, I said, "Can you talk, Ronald?"
Getting my meaning, he answered, "Yes, I'm in the hall."
"Good, listen. Do you remember the games that we used to play at your place after school?"
"You bet I do."
"Are you up for it tonight? If you're game, we can go the whole way."
"Dave, I can't wait," he said, hurriedly, his voice dripping with anticipation. "Give me a couple of hours. I'll have some tea, soak in a hot bath, and then I'll be with you."
"OK," I replied, "and Ronald?"
"Yes?"

"Make sure that you have a good soak, won't you?" My words laced with insinuation, the meaning clear to him.

He chuckled and replied, "Of course, you too."

By this time, almost salivating, I said, "Be prepared for a late night, Ronald."

"The later the better. Do you know, Dave, I've never forgotten our after school sessions and hoped that you'd get back in touch one day," he said quietly, as he replaced the receiver without giving me the chance to reply.

Sitting in the living room, I sipped a glass of scotch and half-listened to the Mozart Clarinet Concerto, pleasantly tipsy, my mind filled with erotic images. I jumped up and almost ran to the front door as I heard the car pull up outside. He stood in front of me and smiled, both of us slightly older, two nineteen-year-old gay boys, very glad of each other's company. He later told me that he too felt both lonely and isolated, but for that night, none of it mattered. As I closed the front door, he looked at me, put his arms around my neck, and we gave each other a long, deep kiss. I led him into the sitting room, revelling in the privacy of it all, as we fell onto the settee hungry for each other.

"Let's get rid of these clothes," he murmured, and we undressed each other. At that moment, I felt neither guilt nor any sense of being dirty or queer. Naked, we made love in the lounge, and then moved to a bedroom, until finally, covered in sweat, we fell exhausted into each other's arms and slept.

Ronald left the house at about three o'clock in the morning and drove away. I never saw him again. As for myself, I spent the day in a grotty, back street pub getting drunk, my guilt and self-loathing back with full force. I looked around at the rough working men as they supped their pints, their copies of *The Daily Mirror* open at the racing page sticking out of their pockets, and wondered what they would think of me if they knew what I'd been doing the previous evening. In my heart I knew the answer.

One night, shortly after this incident, a group of us came back from a night out in Watchet. As usual we were all three parts pissed and in good humour. As we entered the darkened barrack block, none too quietly, a voice quietly called my name. It had a silky quality, and as I approached the bed space a feeling of unease flowed through me. "Yes?" I said, tentatively.

"Hello, Dave," the disembodied voice continued, "we haven't met. I'm Brian, and a very good friend of Ken's. Perhaps we can have a talk tomorrow?"

A feeling of utter dread overcame me as I turned to ice and wanted to vomit. I answered quietly, "Yes, of course." I turned and walked slowly towards my bed. I slept little that night.

Brian and Ken had met as pupils at The Royal Military School of Music, Kneller Hall. The reason that I didn't know Brian was because he'd started his course as I'd just arrived in Germany and our paths hadn't crossed. Ken, on the other hand, had been sent directly to the School of Music straight from boys' service and had fallen, almost literally, into the arms of Brian. Reading between the lines, I gathered that the two of them had become lovers and had discussed me in great detail. To be honest, I found Brian repulsive. There was something menacing about him and I didn't find him in the slightest bit attractive. Was it a case of my seeing myself in him and not liking what I saw? Perhaps Ken thought that he was doing me a favour by providing me with a ready-made lover? I don't know, but I do know that I didn't fancy him in the slightest and did my best to avoid him. I now realise, of course, that Brian mirrored myself. He was a homosexual, just like me, and I was terrified of being found guilty by association. Looking back, I admire him in a way. He wasn't overtly gay and never flaunted his sexuality, but at the same time he never hid it either.

Brian was a little ahead of his time. When I began to realise that he meant me no harm I became less cautious and more relaxed when I was with him. The truth is that he fancied me and at the same time understood my problems. In his way, he tried to help me, but I was having none of it. I remember that he once asked me to visit him at his parents' home in Birmingham, and that I turned him down. If, on the other hand, I'd have found him sexually attractive, then it would have been a different story – but as I mentioned earlier, no-one fancies everyone.

I clearly remember an incident on a train journey back from a weekend leave. Brian and I were sitting alone in a compartment; he was reading a copy of *The Sunday Times* colour supplement. Homosexuality had just been legalised between consenting adults and there was a large spread on the subject. Leaning across, Brian offered the magazine and said, "Read that." Reluctantly I took it and read the sentence indicated. It was from a public schoolboy who said, "Homosexuality, worry about it? Of course not, I just lie back and enjoy it." Those words have stuck in my mind to this day. As I handed the magazine back, Brian looked at me and said, "Perhaps you should take that advice, Dave?" I said nothing, and looked guiltily through the window.

Because the regiment was from the Midlands, we were offered cheap return coach fares to and from Birmingham for the weekend. Brian and I often took advantage them. The return journey was always late on a Sunday night and we'd sit together, covering ourselves with an overcoat and pretending to sleep. A mutual masturbation session went on between us in the dark of the coach as it trundled back towards Somerset. I couldn't help it. Slowly but surely, Brian was starting to wear my resistance down. After all, we all need sexual contact, don't we? And contact with Brian was better than no contact at all.

At around about this time I took over the running of the band club. I was in heaven, surrounded by all that booze, and had the extreme luxury of my own room attached to the bar. The band club was in a separate building, just by the band practice room, and was totally separated from the rest of the billets, ensuring privacy. On the night of this incident, the bar was closed. The next day we were due what was known as a 'Kneller Hall Inspection', probably the most important date in any army musician's calendar. The inspection was to be carried out by the most senior director of music in the British Army, at that time, Lt/Colonel 'Jiggs' Jaeger. One of the most famous of all of the army directors of music of recent times, the man was a legend. To say that we were all nervous would be to underestimate the case. Brian, knowing that the club would be closed and that I'd be alone, took advantage of the situation. I was sitting on the edge of my bed bulling my boots when he walked in and sat next to me. "Shall I lock the door?" he asked, as I nodded, saying nothing. I suppose that it was inevitable sooner or later. The pressure over a period of months, coupled with my anxiety of the following day's inspection, just made me cave in. I wasn't raped – to say that I was would be a lie and a gross distortion of the truth. I just lay there and let him get on with it, feeling no particular pleasure or satisfaction. After it was over, Brian left, and I got on with bulling my boots.

The next day, while the bandmaster was conducting the test piece closely watched by Jeager, I had a few bars rest and thought to myself, "You had sex last night, and here you are playing the overture to 'Iolanthe' in front of the most senior musician in the army." I glanced across at Brian. He had the audacity to look at me, smile and give me wink, his face full of triumph. I couldn't help myself as I thought, "You cheeky bastard," and returned his smile. Where this would have all led to I don't know, but one day shortly afterwards, fate was to take a hand.

I can see it to this day – almost surreal, as if Brian and I were the only two people left on earth, and everyone else had mysteriously disappeared. He was standing alone – I don't think that I've ever seen a more forlorn figure, and I knew instantly that something was wrong, as if he'd lost someone very dear to him. I approached him and said quietly, "Are you alright, Brian?"

He laughed, bitterly as he replied, "Alright? No I'm not. I've just had a visit from the SIB (The Army Special Investigation Branch, the CID of the military police). I've got to go with them."

"Oh, Christ," I muttered, "What happened?"

"Nothing," he said noncommittally, his face white.

I didn't know what to say as I looked at this utterly dejected young man uneasily. To my everlasting shame, unable to meet his gaze, I said, "Good luck," and walked away, wanting to put as much space between us as possible. I never saw him again. He disappeared, almost as if he'd never existed

Many years later I was to discover that he'd been charged with a serious sexual assault against a twelve year old girl and been handed over to the civil police. Our relationship was a strange one. In his way I think that he tried to help me and totally understood my predicament. But I was too frightened to become too closely associated with him. The fear of discovery lived with me constantly and, as I said earlier, guilt by association is a very powerful force when you're in the position that I was in at that time.

Just before the Kneller Hall Inspection, our bandmaster, Jim Parkinson was court-martialled for the embezzlement of army funds. He was always in debt and had been fiddling the band accounts. Found guilty, he was dismissed from the service and dishonourably discharged. At the same time they got rid of the band Staff Sergeant. The role of the most senior NCO in the band is largely one of administration and discipline. He can be anything from a sergeant to a WO2, Sergeant Major. As far as the army was concerned, he should have known what was going on and done something about it. So they got rid of him as well and he took early retirement. A classic case of guilt by association.

The band was taken over by one of the finest men that I've ever known, BM Freddie Fitch. I adored that man and will never forget him. Prior to joining us he'd been the bandmaster of an African regiment, The Malawi Rifles. Later, he was to go on to become one of the most senior directors of music in the British Army, but for the next few years he was our boss. Freddie liked me, but often used to say, "Blast you, Spencer, blasted idiot," after I'd managed to play a B flat, rather than a B natural. As the first clarinet stand was directly in front of the conductor and Freddie never wore a watch, I'd hang mine over the front of the stand, otherwise we'd always be late for lunch. The musical standard of the band soared with the arrival of Freddie Fitch and we at last started to play some good music.

That winter, just before Christmas, we went up to Sutton Coldfield to do a concert with the boys' band, in Birmingham's Central Hall. I remember walking into my old barrack room, as the memories of my own boys' service came flooding back. The new generation of boy musicians looked up as I walked in, all of them eager to hear about life in a real band. I was more than happy to oblige as I basked in their unjustified admiration, seeing myself in them just a few short months previously. Freddie and my old friend Kimberly divided the concert programme between them. For the finalé we played Leroy Anderson's, 'A Christmas Festival' – a super firecracker of a piece for that time of the year and a smash hit with the audience.

'Bazz' Starbuck was a trumpet player and the leader of our dance band. His first love was dance band music and he thought of little else, being justifiably proud of the high standard of what he regarded as his own private domain. The band was in great demand and made a good deal of money playing at different functions, usually until the early hours of the morning. They were both versatile and talented. At the time of the Central Hall concert, I took Bazz and some of the other members of his troupe to play with a band that I knew of in Birmingham. To him, anyone who wasn't a dance band musician wasn't a real musician and as I fitted into that category, he looked at me dubiously when I mentioned it.

Just up the road from where the family lived was a grotty little pub that I visited as often as possible. The reason was the barman, Bernie. Bernie, a working class lad, was a few years older than me, in his mid-twenties, and very cute. I often used to drink with a man called 'Paddy' Cornford, whose elderly mother lived just up the road from us. Paddy, a big bluff man, with a drinker's face and a temper to match his name, also happened to be a very good trumpet player. It was he who suggested that the dance band lads might like to join his band for an evening's rehearsal. The rehearsals were held in a large pub in the centre of Birmingham and were very popular. People would come from all over the city just to hear them. I almost felt sorry for Bazz, as he and the others sat down and started to play. To say that these musicians were good is an understatement – they were superb and Bazz and the others struggled to keep up. Don't misunderstand me, our lot didn't disgrace themselves, but they quickly realised that they were playing with real professionals. I howled with laughter at the look on Bazz's face as they took a break and he walked over to me, muttering, "You bastard, Dave. You really dropped us in the shit." It was a great night and Bazz couldn't stop talking about it for months afterwards. To be honest, I've been playing now for over forty years and have never been able to master the intricacies of that type of music. Perhaps that says something about my musical ability – give me a piece of Beethoven any time.

Just after that evening we all went on Christmas leave and I was determined to do something about Bernie, even if it cost me a broken nose. My chance came on Boxing Day night. I'd spent the evening in the pub getting thoroughly pissed and having a knees up with the locals, who all knew and liked me. As closing time approached, I hung back, hoping that John, the licensee, would invite me to stay behind for an after hours drink. My luck was in. We sat drinking and talking for hours, as I regaled them with stories about my army adventures. I was always the life and soul of the party after a few beers. Looking directly into Bernie's eyes, I came onto him outrageously. I was past caring and if anyone did notice, they said nothing. To my great surprise and delight, he didn't seem to mind as I flirted with him. At about two o'clock, the party broke up and Bernie and I found ourselves standing alone on the pavement outside. It was cold, and the wet pavements glinted in the streetlights as I turned towards him, and said, huskily, "Do you want to carry on with the party, Bernie?"

"You bet I do," he replied, "I'm dying for it. But where?"

I hesitated, realising the awful risk that I was about to take, but not giving a damn! "My place?" I suggested.

"But what about your mum and dad?" he said.

"We'll just have to be very quiet, won't we?"

He nodded, and replied, "Fuck it! I'm game if you are. Come on."

Very quietly, we sneaked into the darkened hallway and up the stairs to my bedroom. Closing the door behind me, I turned towards him as he whispered in my ear, "The last one to get undressed is a queer." I chuckled as we both started to get out of our clothes, as quickly as possible.

When I look back at that night and the huge risks we both took, I still shudder with horror. My mother and father were lying almost literally a few feet away and here was I, frolicking about naked in bed with another man. As dawn was breaking we got dressed. I led him down the stairs and let him quietly out into the street. The shed at the bottom of the garden would have been colder, but a bloody sight safer. Even in those early days I was beginning to take risks as the mask started to slip. Just after that the family moved from Birmingham to Redditch and I never saw Bernie again.

This is a good point to answer a few questions. There is absolutely no doubt in my mind that both Bernie and Ronald were gay and just as lonely and isolated as I was. Why then didn't I cultivate the friendships and carry on seeing them? It would have been the perfect solution to all of our problems. I wasn't in love with either of them, but we were physically attracted to each other, so why not carry on? We were young men and to be frank, needed sexual contact. The answer is as simple as it is sad. I was so riddled with guilt after having sex with them that I never wanted to set eyes on them again.

The summer was my favourite time as an army musician. It was during the summer months that we were at our most active, giving concerts and marching displays all over the country, including the popular bandstands at the seaside during the summer months. Above all, we loved doing agricultural shows, because there was always a beer tent and we'd spend all of our time between displays or concerts sinking pints. However, I never remember an occasion when a member of the band was too drunk to do his job.

I was so happy. We'd spend weeks away from the barracks and literally live out of suitcases. Of course, we weren't given hotel accommodation, and would normally stay at the nearest army base. As long as we had a good pub, and a fish and chip shop or Chinese restaurant to visit after the pub closed, we were happy. They were relaxing days, as we could generally lie in bed the next morning, normally not being needed until late morning.

School concert tours were amongst my favourites. We'd tour around different schools in one area, usually giving a concert in the morning and another in the afternoon. The kids were always an enthusiastic audience and gave us a great welcome; whether that's because they were missing lessons, or genuinely enjoyed the music, I don't know. I suspect a bit of both. Bazz Starbuck had a party piece that always went down well. He'd play the 'Post Horn Gallop', first on the post horn, swapping half way through to an old .303 rifle. The bore on the .303 is the exact length as that of the post horn, and all that was needed was a mouth piece. This was always a smash hit and brought the house down.

Our time wasn't only spent in England. We had a wild adventure in France at one time, the locals being extremely hospitable and welcoming. One night, after consuming large amounts of vino, we staggered back to camp. I was with Frank Gladding, Mo Pinner and Harry Dennick. As we crossed the Town Square, Frank glanced up at a French tricolour flying from a tall flagpole and decided that it would make a good souvenir for the band club. If he'd been sober, he'd probably have broken his neck as he ascended the pole. We stood at the base and urged him on gleefully. Harry happened to glance over at the corner of the square and saw two gendarmes slowly approaching. Abandoning poor Frank, we legged it around the nearest corner and watched the events unfold. As the two policemen walked quietly over, Frank shouted, in triumph, "I've got the bastard, lads." The three of us looked on, howling with laughter, as Frank proceeded to descend, straight into the arms of the waiting policemen. The bigger of the two muttered something incomprehensible and pointed his finger under Frank's nose, before tucking the flag under his arm and walking away, closely followed by his colleague.

"You bunch of wankers," shouted Frank, as he staggered towards us, scowling. "You could have warned me." Maurice encircled Frank's shoulder with his arm and said, tipsily and with the utmost seriousness, "Frank, you'll go down in army band folk lore for what you've just done." A huge grin spread across Frank's face, as he replied, eagerly, "Do you really think so, Maurice. Do you?" Maurice leered drunkenly, his face looking positively evil, as he replied, "Oh, yes, Frank." We made our way back to barracks and fell into bed.

On a more serious note, we took part in the 25th anniversary of the celebrations for the D-Day landings in France, an experience that I'll never forget – the old veterans standing proudly on parade, their medals glinting in the sun, while with bowed heads they remembered their fallen comrades. I was to be present on another D-Day parade exactly five years later and it would be the last time that I'd ever be with my regiment.

Two of the best friends that I've ever had in my life served with me in those days – John Davis, known universally as 'Dob', and Joe Wilson. They were both good mates and deserve a mention here. I spoke to John recently about the old times and he said something very interesting to me. "Do you know," he said, "We just shrugged our shoulders at your strange little ways and said to ourselves, 'Well, that's just Dave, isn't it?'" On many occasions, coming back from some pub or other, I'd want to unburden myself to him, but could never quite pluck up sufficient courage. As for Joe, he too was a good friend. I tracked him down some years ago, but sadly he wouldn't get back in contact. He and I did a great deal of drinking together over the years, and they will appear in the story again.

It was at this time that I was to be given the nickname that still haunts me to this day, 'Spanner'. One morning, I was walking with some of the lads down to 'Mrs T's' for a cup of tea and a roll. Mrs T was a delightful old lady, who would appear every morning driving an old *Morris Minor*. She had a wooden kiosk that she'd been running since the war and was in direct competition with the NAAFI. She and a friend would set up shop and start serving. She was like a typical Women's Institute member, and reminded me of Miss Marple and called everyone 'dear'. Anyway, as we were walking towards the kiosk, someone from the Corps of Drums called across to me, "Eh, Spenner!" thinking that Spenner was my name, not

Spencer. Now, us snotty musicians, contemptuously called the members of the drum corps, 'Bandsmen with their brains kicked in', as they weren't the brightest of lads (although that sounds very pretentious). They would often play with the band on parade and were a good crowd. They were all trained soldiers and had their role to play within the regiment. Terry Baxter thought that this was highly amusing and forever afterwards called me 'Spenner', and over a period of time this became 'Spanner', and has stuck with me ever since.

In about the summer of 1968 I was involved in an accident that nearly cost my companions and myself our lives and I believe that I was to blame. A few days previously, the band had given a concert in Lynmouth, on the other side of Exmoor, *Lorna Doone* country. On the way back, some of our lads were driving in a private car and had an accident, ending up in hospital. Harry Dennick, a lad called Andrew, and I borrowed a powerful sports car from someone in the corps of drums and drove back over the moor to Lynmouth. It's very wild country and can be dangerous driving at night if you're not careful. Of course, the inevitable happened, and Andrew and I got smashed. On the way back Harry lost control of the car and we left the road, smashing into a tree. If we'd have come off that road a few yards earlier, I wouldn't be sitting here writing this today, as there were sheer cliffs and the rocks far below were jagged and deadly. The emergency services were called out and we were taken to the same hospital as the other lads in Taunton.

I have no real memory of that night, as I was badly concussed and suffered a fractured sternum. When we were discharged from the hospital, we were sent home on a week's sick leave, much to the anger of the BM, who found himself short of five musicians at the busiest time of the year. A few days later, Harry and his wife called round to our house in Church Street and asked to see me. We all went up to the pub and had a pint. Harry was unusually serious and asked if I realised that it was me who was responsible for the accident. My mouth fell open in shock, as he went on to explain that I'd become aggressive towards Andrew and had taken a swing at him. My punch had missed Andrew and hit Harry on the back of the head, causing him to lose control of the car.

To this day, I still don't know if that's what happened. I would only say that I never became violent after I'd been drinking. Dad took me to see a lawyer from the *AA* for some advice, which I never needed, as nothing ever came of it.

Andrew was a nice lad, darkly handsome with brown eyes and an infectious grin. He eventually married a lovely girl whom I adored. If I'd been straight, she would have been the type that I would have fallen for. I still have a ring that once belonged to her and often wear it to this day. Sadly, Andrew was also to leave the army under a cloud at about the same time as me. I recently tried to contact him, but never received a reply. This is something that's happened quite often over the years.

Remembering Paul and Patrick, the barman from the 'Egremont' in Williton, I still very much fancied Paul and would have done anything to get involved with him. One evening, a group of us were in the band club getting drunk as usual. Maurice, who didn't like Paul, mentioned that Paul and Patrick often spent time together down on the beach late at night. He looked knowingly at us and said, "One thing's for sure, they're not looking at the moon."

My ears went up and, like a coward, I sneered along with the rest of them, but in my heart, I was green with envy. I would gladly have got together with either but it was not to be. I must be perfectly honest and say that how much truth there was in Maurice's story is impossible for me to tell.

One of our favourite watering holes in Watchet was the *British Legion Club*. The attraction was the cheap and lethal cider, a bargain at just one shilling a pint. Myself, John, Joe and Andrew would often spend time in there getting quietly drunk.

The barman was a man called Frank, whose aged father would sit up in the corner looking like a wrinkled old prune, contentedly puffing away on his pipe. The old boy must have been at least 90 years old. Frank was a bachelor and on more than one occasion invited me to stay behind after closing time. I can't be sure of his motive, as he never made a move on me. I do know that Andrew was also often invited to stay behind after everyone else had left – whether anything went on between the two of them, I just don't know. Many years later, I went back to Watchet and walked into a pub. Sure enough, there was Frank serving behind the bar, and he hadn't changed a bit in the intervening years. I immediately noticed, as I walked in, that he had a small group of good-looking young teenage boys with him, all laughing and joking together. By this time, of course, I was much more savvy and knew the score. To the unknowing eye, it would probably have meant nothing, but to me, it spoke volumes. As I walked towards the bar, I looked over at the group and hoped that Frank would introduce me to some of them, once I'd made myself known to him. At first I said nothing and just ordered a pint. Frank made no show of recognising me. After a while, I said, "Hello, Frank. You don't remember me, do you?" "Oh but I do, Sir," he replied. Frank called everyone, 'Sir'.

I was just preparing myself for an afternoon of drinking and, hopefully, an introduction, when two men walked in. They had police written all over them. Frank looked up as they approached and his face fell. One of the men spoke to him quietly and flashed a warrant card, and Frank nodded, as if facing the inevitable. He turned, picked up his jacket and without looking at me walked out, closely followed by the two policemen. The boys at the bar had fallen silent as their eyes followed Frank's retreating back. The age of consent for gay men was still 21 at that time, and if Frank had been involved with any of those boys, then he was in big trouble. I drank my pint and left. On that visit, as I was walking around, my mind occupied by thoughts of my years spent there with the army, I saw a woman that I recognised. She remembered me and smiled sadly. I'd read in a national newspaper, some months previously, that a young sergeant from my old regiment had been killed. His name was David and I remembered that he'd married this lady's daughter. I can see him now, a tall, slim young man with brown hair and gentle manner. We conversed for a while and I offered her my condolences. As I walked away, my heart was filled with sadness at such a tragic waste of a young life. All the pleasure disappeared from the afternoon and I took the next bus back to Taunton.

On Saint George's Day, 23rd April 1968, in the presence of Field Marshal Montgomery of Alamein, the Royal Warwickshire Fusiliers disappeared into the archives of military history and the second battalion of the Royal Regiment of Fusiliers was born. We changed our distinctive gold and blue hackle for the white and red one of the new regiment. I was of course on parade that day, the regimental band playing a central and important part in the proceedings.

Musical life went on just the same as ever and we spent time in rehearsal for our various concerts and performances under the baton of Freddie Fitch, who continued to say, "Blast you, Spencer," from time to time. One day we were informed that the whole battalion was to go to France, including the band. As a trip abroad was always to be welcomed, our thoughts turned to wine and French composers. The regiment embarked onto a military troop carrier called the 'Sir Tristram' and we headed across the English Channel. We were greeted at the quayside by a number of French police motorcyclists, riding very powerful machines indeed. I've never seen anything like it, as we set off in a long, snaking convoy and the police roared up and down the column like a swarm of angry bees. They shot ahead at incredible speed, screeching to a halt at every crossroads and imperiously stopping the traffic as we sped past. This seemed to go on forever until we at last slowed and stopped, the khaki vehicles strung along the side of the road like a sleeping snake. "Half an hour's break," some one shouted, as we descended into the humid evening air and looked around.

As luck would have it, we'd stopped outside a grocer's shop, which we soon discovered (this being France) had shelves full of bottles of wine. We happily sat at the side of the road munching baguettes and discreetly drinking red wine. One of the squaddies spotted us as he walked past, and said, with a grin, "Trust the fucking band to find the booze. Give us a swig, mate." I was glad to oblige, as he looked around secretively, before he took a large and long drink, the level of the bottle going down alarmingly. "Thanks, pal," he said, before quickly heading over towards his truck and climbing aboard. I laughed as I realised that he was one of the drivers. Soon we were speeding off into the sunset, our journey far from over. We arrived in the early hours of the morning at the French equivalent of Catterick, an army barracks that must have been in use since the time of Napoleon.

Mourmelon-le-Grand is set in the Champagne region of France and I remember it to this day with affection. The locals opened their arms to us, as if they'd been liberated all over again, and we soon found our favourite watering hole. *Le Café du Commerce* was situated at the far end of the small town, just by the church and we literally took it over. We were there at the height of the summer and I remember how humid and hot it was. Many a day and night the band spent in that bar between concerts, eating large, thick ham baguettes and drinking ice cold beer. People like Harvey Smith and John Davis were in their element, having the benefit of 'O' Level French, while the rest of us managed to get along quite well without it, thank you very much. The owner was a lovely girl called Ida, who always made us welcome and whose profits must have soared during the weeks that we were there. We toured the countryside, no matter how small the hamlet – if it had a bandstand, then we'd play there. Afterwards, there would be speeches from the mayor, lots of embracing and gallons of Champagne. One of the highlights of our visit was a concert that we gave on the steps of the medieval cathedral at Rheims. At the end of each concert, we would always play the two National Anthems, the patriotic French singing the words to theirs with gusto.

Because Mourmelon is a garrison town, there were many French soldiers around. One day, as I was walking out of the barracks in the direction of the centre, I spotted a young French conscript staggering towards me, loaded down with a rifle and equipment. The poor boy looked exhausted as I shouted encouragement to him in a language that he couldn't understand. He was on his last legs, but managed a smile and a nod as he went past. I was always very correct on passing a French army officer, making sure that I saluted as we showed each other mutual respect.

One day, Harvey, myself and Mike Faulding managed to fall foul of not only the bandmaster, but of the RSM as well. Harvey had met two young French soldiers, and being able to speak the language they'd become good friends. Let me tell you, these two were absolutely gorgeous, and like most of their race, very laid back. I just sat and drooled over them as we sipped a glass of red wine, not understanding a word of what they said, but quite content to look. It was early evening and they invited us to their mess for dinner, an invitation that we gladly accepted.

The mess that they took us to was far better than ours, and that should have set alarm bells off in our heads. For a start, there was waiter service and the three of us looked at each other, anxiously, as we realised that something was wrong. "Oh, Christ," I heard Harvey mutter, as he looked over my head. "Don't turn around," he whispered urgently, "It's the BM with the RSM." Too late, we realised that we were dining in the sergeant's mess and we could do nothing about it. That was the longest meal of my life – the BM and RSM studiously avoided making any eye contact, while the two young sergeants chattered away, unaware of our difficult situation.

At one point, we even hoped that we hadn't been spotted. Some hope. We finally finished, left and awaited our fate.

The next morning we were summoned by a very irate Freddie, who gave us the biggest bollocking of our lives and demanded that we explain ourselves. Mike and I left it to poor old Harvey to do the talking and he did very well. We had no idea that those two were sergeants, he explained, which was true. By the time we realised, it was too late, and we could hardly get up and walk out. "Could we, Sir?" he said, hopefully. Freddie calmed down a bit and muttered something about, "In the circumstances, but don't you dare let it happen again. Blasted idiots!" We counted our blessings and beat a hasty retreat.

Sadly, all good things must come to an end, and we finally returned to Watchet, our French sojourn over.

Over the years, I've spoken fondly to Martin of our time in Mourmelon. A couple of years ago, we spent a happy weekend in Rheims and Martin suggested that we stop off and take a look at the place on our way back to Luxembourg. As we pulled up, all the memories came flooding back. We found the café and entered. Nothing seemed to have changed, as we sat down, saying good day to the three old gentlemen sitting opposite. I didn't recognise the woman who came to serve us; after all it had been a very long time. Martin ordered two coffees and asked if we could have two sandwiches to take with us when we left. She said, "Of course," and walked into the back of the bar. I turned to the old men, and said, in good but accented French, that I'd been there with the British army many years previously. They were very interested, as I told them of our visit and the good times that we'd had. When Ida returned (yes it was her), she looked at me with amazement. "Of course I remember," she said, "Especially Harvey and Richard." She looked at me closely, and said, "So, you're David?"

"Yes," I replied, "I'm the one that every one called stupid because I spoke no French."

She laughed and said, "Not any more."

We spent an hour or two talking about those times, and after having our photograph taken together we said our fond farewells. Ida and I exchange cards every Christmas and I've promised myself a return visit one day. After all it's only just down the road.

The band sat facing the audience, a sea of red poppies, regimental blazers and gleaming rows of medals. The standard-bearers stood to attention, their flags held stiffly upright as they stared straight ahead. Overhead, the lights beat down illuminating the stage, as the band and orchestra waited. Our dark blue No 1 dress uniforms, with the wide red stripe of the infantry down each leg, contrasted with the evening dress of the orchestral players of the Birmingham Symphony Orchestra, as we waited. The conductor, Harold Gray, walked on to the stage and mounted the rostrum. Looking around, he lifted his baton, as the band fanfare trumpeters brought their long, brass instruments to their lips and waited, the light glinting off the surface of the highly polished trumpets. Gray smiled, nodded, and with a flick of his right wrist the long, white stick came down. The grand march from the Verdi opera *Aida* opened the 1968 Festival of Remembrance. Never in my widest dreams would I have thought that one day, I would be sitting on the stage playing with that fine orchestra.

I'll never forget the concert and service that followed. The standard-bearers of the Royal British Legion came from all over the Midlands. These men and women stood with pride and remembered their fallen comrades as they solemnly lowered the flags during the playing of the 'Last Post'. We played the fine 'Pomp and Circumstance' march No 1 by Edward Elgar, the audience singing the patriotic words with gusto. Freddie Fitch led the community singing, with such favourites as 'We'll Meet Again' and 'Roll Out The Barrel' as the people joined in and sang their hearts out.

Sitting in the audience that night was a 16-year-old boy, his name, Martin. Tall and slim, with wavy, light brown hair, he sat and watched the military musicians with interest. I had no idea that he was there. I couldn't possibly have known. He was just one of many in the town hall that night. In 1976 we were to meet, fall in love and settle down together in a long and happy relationship. If only I could have had the gift of seeing into the future, perhaps the ordeal that was to come later would have been more bearable, knowing that I would, at last, find real happiness.

A lad called Steven and I slept together. He was a member of the band and not particularly popular. He meant absolutely nothing to me, but was there and willing, so why not? Our sexual encounter was unsatisfactory and transient. It wouldn't be worth mentioning, but for one thing – it cost me a great deal of money. As is so often the case, Steven didn't like the side of himself that he was shown on the night of our sex together, and so decided to kill the messenger.

Late one Friday night, after an evening on the town celebrating his 21st birthday, he came back to the barracks drunk. I needed a pee, climbed out of bed and walked across the road in my pyjamas and into the toilet block. Steven saw me and followed. He was a big, muscular lad and spoiling for a fight. I don't remember what he said, but I do remember the thick lip that he gave me as he smashed his fist into my face. I fell to the floor as he walked away. After a while, in a daze, I staggered into the barracks, my upper lip pouring with blood. My roommates saw my state and came to help. They were horrified – only squaddies behaved in that way. I cleaned myself up and went back to bed.

Very early the next morning, Steven came into my room and knelt by the side of my bed, apologising, over and over. I believe that he was genuinely sorry for his actions and I was quite ready to forgive him and forget about the matter, after all, these things do happen, and the only thing that was really injured was my pride. However, there was a problem. My lip was badly swollen and we had an important concert that day at Dunster Castle. None of this could have happened at a worse time, and I didn't know what to do. One of the lads suggested that I go and see the band sergeant, Frank Smith. Reluctantly, I walked over to the married quarters, which were quite a distance from the camp, and knocked on the front door. Frank's wife, Betty, opened it and looked at me, her face creased with horror. "Oh, Dave," she said, "What on earth's happened to you?"

I smiled lopsidedly and winced, "Hello, Betty. Is Frank there?"
"Come on in, love. I'll make you a cup of tea," she said, ushering me in, and calling up the stairs, "Frank, Frank! Dave Spencer's here. Come down, his face is in a right mess."

Frank walked into the living room, took one look at me, and said, gruffly, "Bloody hell, brother, what's happened to you?" Frank, called everyone 'brother', just like an old time evangelist. Frank Smith was a tall, thin man, with a craggy, lived-in face and a heart of gold. I explained the situation to him, saying, "Look, Frank, there's no way that I can play this afternoon with this lip." "Bugger your bloody lip, Dave. I want to speak to..." he said, "come with me." Frank was angry and it was a bad idea to cross him. I said nothing as we climbed into his car and drove over to the barracks. As soon as we arrived, he walked into Steven's billet, placed him under arrest and marched him straight down to the guardhouse.

If Steven had have been more popular, I've no doubt that things could have been smoothed over. But Frank was adamant that he should be charged and nothing would change his mind. As this was a Saturday, I'd have to now stay behind

95

until Monday to give evidence against him and I was very annoyed.

On Monday morning we all congregated outside the company commander's office and waited. By this time, I was beginning to feel sorry for Steven and foolishly decided that if I could, I'd try and help him. Frank and I marched in to the office and saluted. As is usual in military law, Steven had his hat and belt removed and was marched in at double time. The company commander, a major, asked me what had happened. I gave a watered down account of events, trying to make it seem less serious than it had been. Out of the corner of my eye, I could see a look of horror pass over Frank's face. It was obvious to everyone that I was lying. The OC lifted his hand and said, quietly, "I would remind you that you're under oath and you're not telling me the truth. Now, start again and don't leave anything out." I muttered, "Yes, Sir," and gave a true account of the evenings events.

The OC looked at Steven, and said, "I find you guilty of common assault. Do you accept my punishment?"
"Yes Sir," said Steven, knowing that to say no would have meant a higher court and perhaps a higher sentence.
"28 days!" he snapped, before turning his eyes towards me and saying, "As for you, you've committed perjury and I'm going to charge you under the army act with that crime. Sergeant Major," he said to the CSM, "Write out the charge sheet and I'll deal with it now."

Steven was marched out to start 28 days as a prisoner in the guardroom and I, now the prisoner, was marched back in again, this time minus my hat and belt. I was found guilty as charged and fined a month's loss of pay. The severity of Steven's punishment shocked me – I'd expected that he would be hit in the pocket, but to be sent to jail for a month came as a surprise. I've no way of knowing what was said between Frank Smith and the OC prior to my going in to give evidence, but I suspect that Frank had really laid down the poison. As for me, I left for a walking (and drinking) holiday with John Davis on the Isle of Skye, while Steven was left to languish inside the prison. That was the most expensive sex that I've ever had. I climbed aboard the train to Scotland a lot poorer, but not much wiser, and John and I got thoroughly drunk on the way.

One time when the band was on tour in the Manchester area, Frank Smith decided that he wanted to visit the then notorious district of Moss Side, and a number of us agreed to go along. We piled into a taxi and found an illegal drinking den where we had a whale of a time, finally staggering out of the place in the early hours of the morning.

Frank and Bazz Starbuck were like a double act. Frank tall and thin, Bazz short and fat, just like Laurel and Hardy, and they both played the situation for all it was worth. The various occupants of this drinking club, a really rough bunch, looked on in bemusement as they went through their routine like a couple of old pro's. We finally left swearing eternal friendship and promising to return one day, as the locals, most of them ex-cons from Strangeways Prison, saw us off. Frank was heard to mutter to Bazz as we climbed into the taxi, "Go back there – you must be joking, brother."

In October of 1969 we packed our kit and prepared to leave Watchet for our next posting, Berlin. I stood outside the band club one day and watched as a number of familiar faces from the past came into sight. There was Andy, Phillip and my old friend and would-be lover, Peter. The four of us had been on boys' service together and knew each other well. We all shook hands as Peter introduced me to three other lads who were all unfamiliar to me. Bob, Barry and Keith, the latter of whom had curly, blond hair and was so gorgeous that I always fancied him. They'd all been members of The Lancashire Fusiliers. The regiment had been disbanded the previous year when we became The Royal Regiment of Fusiliers, and they weren't best pleased with the situation. Regimental pride plays a big part in anyone's army career, and they felt hard done by at the loss of their regiment. All six of them were good musicians and desperately needed by us. A lot of the old Warwickshire Fusilier band members were coming to the end of their army service and leaving, to be replaced by these hard and gruff Northerners. The band, as I knew it, totally disappeared on their arrival and marked the start of a new era.

Berlin

Trying to continue the lie and not fooling anyone but myself

Up until our departure to Berlin I'd managed to conceal my sexuality well, or so I kidded myself at the time. It was, however, becoming more and more difficult to sustain the lie, and my mental and physical health were beginning to suffer. For six years I'd lived in a state of fear, the fear that any moment my secret would be discovered and that I'd be unmasked. I now know, of course, that my secret wasn't a secret at all, and that everybody knew that I was queer. What's the saying, 'There's none so blind as those who will not see'? That just about summed me up in those days. If I had allowed myself to think for one minute that they knew, it would have destroyed me. I was a classic case of being 'in denial'. It was a self-defence mechanism that I had to keep hold of at all costs, and the only way to stay sane.

About two years ago, I met Keith for the first time in about thirty years. I asked him, "Keith, did you know about me at the time?" "Dave," he replied, "I knew instantly, and remember saying to the others (the Lancashire Fusiliers), he's queer. I'll lay my life on it."

Keith was both kind and decent to me, and we spent many an hour drinking in a little kiosk near the barracks. I remember spending a very happy Christmas with him and his wife during our first year in Berlin. After lunch and a great deal of boozing, Keith decided that he needed to go and sleep it off for a while. I, too, had had more than my fair share and asked innocently if I could join him. He grinned and said, "Yes. But keep your hands to yourself, my boy." It was said in a not unpleasant or unfriendly way, but the message was clear. Not that I would have dared to lay a finger on him, because if I had, the reaction would have been very violent, and I knew it.

There were other things that I preferred to ignore. There was one two-man room in the band accommodation, and one of the occupants decided to move out, so I quickly said that I wanted to take his place. A lad called John, who I must say was very cute (that wasn't my reason for wanting to move in), was the other person sharing the room. When he discovered that it was me who wanted to replace his roommate, he, too, decided that he wanted a change of scenery and quickly moved out. There was no way that he was going to share with me. That should have told me something, but, believe it or not, I chose to ignore it. However, my old friend, Peter, had no such qualms and quickly moved in with me. We happily shared that room for two years. After all, he had no fear of me and had known all about my sexuality for years.

Another incident that I remember well was the time that Bob Shaw told me graphically and in great detail about two gays in the Lancashires, who had been caught in bed together and had to be separated by having a bucket of cold water thrown over them.

I also came on to two of the other lads during our time in Berlin, to no avail, of course. But did I really believe that they said nothing to anybody else? I'm sure that I kidded myself that they said nothing, although that was totally unrealistic.

So, what saved me? I was popular and as long as I didn't flaunt myself too much; I think that it was a case of live and let live. The nearest I ever came to be labelled queer was when one of the more aggressive of the ex-Lancashire Fusiliers told me that I was like a big girl. I'm sure that there could have been a violent reaction from one or two of these Lancashire lads on more than one occasion, but something held them back and, to be honest, I don't know what it was.

No, the only thing that I could do was to put my head in the sand, keep it there and hope for the best. As you'll see later, it could have been a very different story, as my old sparring partner Steven was to find out to his cost.

West Berlin – what a place it was in 1969 at the height of the 'Cold War'; a small island surrounded by a sea of hostility and us in the middle of it, like something out of a John Le Carré novel, only this was for real. It was an exciting place to be and was by far the best posting that I ever had. Berlin was truly a city of spies and intrigue, dominated by the wall and the grey, uniformed Stassi as they sat on the other side watched over by their Russian masters.

"This telephone is not secure!" was the message in every office in the barracks, while outside, black Russian cars cruised the streets looking for any clue to our strengths and weaknesses. In a word, spying. We of course did the same along with our American and French allies. It was like a big game of hide and seek, with everyone joining in.

We were told on arrival that in the event of hostilities breaking out, we would get no help from the West and could expect either death, or imprisonment. We were a long way behind the 'Iron Curtain' and totally isolated. Just like me!

The attitude of the Berliners was live for today, because tomorrow you may well be dead. Many of them remembered clearly what had happened to them when the Russians had arrived in 1945 and they didn't want to repeat the experience.

There was a thriving and vibrant gay scene, which for me may just as well have been on Mars. Even had I dared to contemplate the idea of exploring this delightful underworld, I would have quickly dismissed the notion out of hand. Without sounding melodramatic, the Russians were always looking out for people like me, and don't think for one minute that because of my lowly position they would have had no interest in me. I would have very quickly been enticed into a 'Honey Trap' and ensnared. There were many other intelligence agencies at work in that city and I would have been quite a catch for any of them. For me, Berlin was a time of enforced celibacy, whether I liked it or not. I was a young man full of testosterone and at the peak of my sexual desires, and, to be honest, the sexual frustration was almost unbearable – not for me a trip to a prostitute in town to relieve my urges, as many soldiers did.

There are two instances of my need for some kind of sexual contact during that time. There was a lad, 'Barry', who sent me signals that I misread in a big way. I realise now that at best he was being mischievous, or at worst, very unkind. We had a television in the band club and I would often lean over the back of a settee and watch it. Whenever Barry saw me doing this, he'd come up to the side of me, stand very close and bend over, so that our shoulders were touching. He'd say nothing but would rub his leg up and down against mine – something that I found highly exciting. If Barry had been gay, this would have been a strong sexual signal, but of course, he wasn't, and I should have ignored it. Very foolishly, I went to his room one night and made a pass at him, which was totally rejected. Needless to say I had been drinking and should have known better. How I was able to look him in the face the next day I just don't know. And here was me kidding myself that no one knew anything about my sexuality. He never mentioned the incident again to me, but what he said behind my back is another matter.

The second incident took place not in Berlin, but Bavaria. Berlin was a claustrophobic place and the army organised trips to overcome the problem. A favourite was skiing and many of us took part. I went on one such trip. We were housed in private homes and I shared a bedroom with a corporal called Alan and a young, attractive soldier. Unusually, because of the cramped accommodation, Alan and I shared the same bed, while the young soldier had a single one. Late one night, after a visit to a local bar, the three of us were lying in bed. Alan, who was naked, started to tease the young soldier by showing him his large erection, and saying, "Come on, you know that you want some of this. Try it, you never know, you might like it." "You're a fucking queer, you are, Alan. Fuck off!" said the young soldier, not taking Alan seriously.

As for me, I wasn't so sure, and would have loved to try it on once the lights were off. I had to decide whether the message was being given for my benefit rather than for the young soldier? It was very tempting. Here was I, lying naked with a rather attractive young man, but dare I make a move? After my experience with Barry, I was ultra cautious and who could blame me? In the end, I decided that it wasn't worth the risk and after a while, drifted off to sleep. It occurred to me recently that that was the only time in the whole of my army career that I ever lay legally in bed with another man.

I now regret not taking advantage of the situation. A long time later, I was to discover that one of the band members owed Alan some money and couldn't pay it back. The bandsman confessed all to me one cold and dark January night, in a watchtower at the Crumlin Road Prison, Northern Ireland, while we were on sentry duty. Apparently, he'd been to see Alan and told him that he couldn't pay him back, and would Alan be prepared to give him more time? Alan had a far better idea. He put it to the young band member, who I knew well and who was highly attractive, extremely well muscled with a smooth olive skin, that there was perhaps another way. Alan, being an NCO, had his own room and therefore plenty of privacy. He said that he would forget the debt for certain favours. The bandsman, who most certainly wasn't gay, saw a way out of his difficulties and readily agreed. From what he told me, Alan certainly made sure that the debt was repaid, with interest. Alan was a very highly regarded NCO and popular with everyone from the CO down. I wonder just how popular he would have been, had they known the truth about him? I think that I know the answer to that question. I liked Alan and the two of us served together as instructors at the depot just before my downfall. I've often wondered what would have happened between us, had I made a move on him that night in Bavaria.

Freddie Fitch left us in Berlin. He'd been promoted and it was a very sad occasion for me. A BM called Rod Parker replaced him. I didn't like Parker and the feeling was mutual. Musically, Berlin was a bit of a desert for us, and from that point of view there's nothing much to say. We did the Queen's birthday parade – fine if you're a spectator, but tedious for us. We also did a huge march past with the Americans and the French, to parade our military might in front of the Russians, but it was even more tedious than the Queen's birthday parade.

However, music played a big part in every Berliner's life. It was the home of one of the finest orchestras in the world, The Berlin Philharmonic Orchestra, and I took advantage of this wonderful musical scene on many occasions. One evening, my mate 'Winnie' (named after 'Winnie the Pooh' because he looked like him) and I went to a performance of Bach's *St Mathew Passion*. Of course, it was fully booked and we couldn't get in. Winnie cursed me roundly and said that he'd warned me. Stung by his words, and not to be out-done, I looked around and wondered if there was any solution. Spying the doorman, who'd obviously been a soldier at some period during his lifetime, I quickly turned to Winnie and said, "Go to the bar and buy three beers and three schnapps."
"What for?" he asked eyeing me with suspicion.
"Just do it, will you, you wanker," I muttered as I sidled over to the old man, smiled and offered him a cigarette.
"Danke," he said, as he looked over at Winnie, who was approaching carefully balancing a tray. His eyes lit up as I

handed him a beer and schnapps. He contentedly took a sip of the schnapps and smiled, looking from one of us to the other. I quickly got to work and using a mixture of 'Pigeon German' and sign language started to try and persuade him to find us some seats. "No. Impossible," he said, shaking his head as I handed over a packet of duty free cigarettes and sent Winnie scuttling towards the bar for some refills.

By this time the performance had started, but that didn't put me off. This pantomime carried on for a while and I knew that my perseverance was beginning to pay off, when, muttering something to himself, he disappeared into an office. He emerged a few seconds later and with a huge, tipsy smile handed over two large cards marked 'Press'. We thanked him profusely, wishing him and his family a long life and good health and death to the Russians, as we made our way back to the bar for another tipple. Triumphantly we walked into the auditorium and found the two press seats. We felt like visiting royalty as we looked around at the beginning of the second part of the oratorio and sat down. The seats were higher than anyone else's and separated from the rest of the audience; it was like sitting in our own private little island. Winnie and I were to spend many happy hours together in that concert hall, but from then on we always made sure that we had tickets.

We once crossed over to the other side of the wall for a night at the opera. Dressed in our dark blue No 1 dress uniforms, we spent the intervals exchanging dirty looks with the Stassi officers, who loathed us to a man, and whose grey uniforms and black jackboots reminded us of another era.

It was at a Gershwin concert that I met an American 'Spook' and his wife. We became very good friends and socialised together on numerous occasions. Harry worked at a huge, top-secret listening-post in the American sector, monitoring Soviet radio traffic. Poor Harry was a prisoner unable to leave West Berlin other than by plane, forbidden to go anywhere near the Russian sector. I never saw him in a uniform and he would always avoid talking about his job, but I suspect that he had a very high rank.

The military train is worth a mention, as it sums up the situation in Berlin to perfection. Each morning, the train would pull out of the station and head through East Berlin towards East Germany. This train was regarded as being British soil, like an embassy on wheels. The doors were locked and the sentries armed, with orders that anyone attempting to enter the train was to be shot on sight. The passengers were equally captive and had to be dressed in uniform. Just after leaving East Berlin, the train would be stopped by soldiers of the occupying power, Russia. The British officer in charge of the train, dressed in his best uniform, would disembark and march towards his Russian counterpart. The two would halt and salute each other, while the British officer handed over the passengers' identity cards. He would then wait, usually pacing up and down, hands behind his back, like Prince Charles. If the Russians were in a good mood, this procedure would be over relatively quickly; if, on the other hand, they weren't, then it could take all day. While this was going on, members of the East German security police and their ferocious dogs would be crawling under the train looking for would-be escapers. Any British soldier foolish enough to stick his head out of the window for a closer look was likely to get it shot off by the Stassi guards. This went on every day, morning going outward, evening coming back. Both the Americans and the French ran their own trains with the same procedures.

One evening we had to do an officers' mess dinner for the allied powers over in Potsdam in the Russian sector of Eastern Germany. Rod Parker had put together a small band, like a chamber orchestra. To get there we had to cross over one of the most famous bridges of modern history into the eastern sector – the 'Glienicker Bridge', as it's known, was a sinister place and often seen in spy films of the period. The bridge was used by the Russians and the allies to hand over each other's captured spies when they'd finished with them. Gary Powers, the American spy-plane pilot, was one of the most famous of these. We were warned that the Russians had the bridge bugged and could hear every word that we said. Someone couldn't resist saying, "That bloke Stalin. What a wanker." Likewise the officers' mess was also bugged, which everyone knew but didn't take any notice of. It was a strange, almost surreal world, the reality of which was far better than any fictional novel.

We did all kinds of crazy things, usually fuelled by copious amounts of alcohol. Peter received a 'Dear John' and decided to get drunk, drinking 22 vodkas in half an hour (and people talk about me). I later found him sitting cross-legged on the floor, his once beautiful French Horn a mangled piece of scrap metal in front of him, after he'd attacked it with a hammer.

Another incident with Andy nearly caused a regimental falling out, after we'd been drinking at lunchtime, and the regiment next door was rehearsing for their regimental day. Their CO was sitting on his horse when Andy, also a horn player, put his instrument through the window and blew it with all his might making the horse bolt. There was absolute hell to pay, but both Peter and Andy got away with it.

As did I on the night that I decided to pay a visit to Rudolph Hess, the Nazi war criminal – the sole prisoner in Spandau prison, which was situated next door to our barracks and guarded in turn by the Russians, Americans, French and British on a rotating three monthly basis. Originally, there were seven Nazi war criminals inside Spandau. They'd been tried at the Nuremberg trials and been sentenced to a various number of years imprisonment. By the time that we arrived in Berlin, Hess was the only prisoner left inside the goal and guarded at huge expense. At various times over the years, it had been suggested that he should be freed, but the Russians were having none of that, and that in his case, life would mean just that – the fact that he remained in the prison gave the

Russians a foothold in the western part of the city and they weren't about to give up that right.

Coming back from a bar after a party one night, drunk out of our minds, I staggered down the driveway towards the prison, as all hell was let loose and lights and alarms went off. Fortunately for me, it was the turn of our French allies to guard the prison, and they didn't realise that I was a British soldier. Some of the lads dragged me back and we merrily made our way home. Now if the Russians had been guarding the prison that night, I shudder to think what might have happened.

Talking of Rudolph Hess gives me an opportunity to mention my old friend Steven who was about to make himself a lot of enemies. We had a lad in the band called John, who'd been an orphan and spent his early life in a home. For some reason Steven took a dislike to John and started to taunt him about his background. That was a big mistake, as John was very popular and Steven wasn't. Instigated by our old friends from the Lancashire Fusiliers, it was decided to 'send him to Coventry' and that's what was done, with devastating effect. Overnight he became a pariah and was totally excluded – things got so bad that he had to have a room to himself as no one would share with him, and he was given the nickname 'Hess', after Rudolph, who, like him, was in solitary confinement. In the end Steven was forced to transfer to another band.

It's an eternal mystery to me why I wasn't on the receiving end of similar treatment. Perhaps I was more popular than I ever thought? I don't suppose that I'll ever know.

To be honest, whether anyone knew about me or not is completely irrelevant, and clouds the issue. My fears were within myself, and no matter how hard I tried, I couldn't come to terms with my homosexuality. The real problem was my denial and until I came to terms with that, nothing would ever change. Against all of the evidence, I still insisted that I wasn't really gay and would one-day wake up and find myself miraculously cured. I shied away from being honest and facing the reality of my situation. Until I did, my life would continue to be unhappy. The problem wasn't the army at all, the real problem lay deep within myself.

In July of 1971 we left Berlin and returned to the UK. Another chapter in my army career was coming to an end and the fateful day ever nearer. It was almost inevitable. I was like a runaway train that was on a collision course and it was all going to end in disaster.

Gathering clouds

Catterick! God how I loathed that place – moors, wind, rain and more rain with countless number of sheep. It had none of the charm of Somerset and suited my mood of deep gloom to perfection, but perhaps I looked at the place with a jaundiced eye. I had served in the army for eight years, with no end in sight and now I'd been posted to this godforsaken spot.

Walking into our allotted accommodation, I looked around in disgust and dropped my suitcase on the floor. "Fucking hell!" I muttered to myself, as I surveyed the eight-man room, a feeling akin to despair engulfing me. After the luxury of our two-man rooms in Berlin, this was indeed a retrograde step. I was, by now, a lance corporal, but as the single occupancy rooms were reserved for the full corporals and the chance of promotion was slight, my chances of getting one of the coveted bunks was a big fat zero. "What can I do?" I thought to myself, an idea beginning to take shape in my mind and growing bigger by the minute. I decided to do some looking around, as soon as I could. Would they allow me to do it? That was the big question.

One morning Parker called me into his office and said that he wanted me to conduct the band at a Sergeants' Mess dinner. I was surprised, as that job usually fell to the senior corporal in the band, something that he wasn't mad about, as he couldn't conduct a bus. It was a chore that he would do anything to avoid. When I told him that I'd been asked to do the job, he smiled, said nothing and lifting his cornet to his mouth blew a few bars of the 'Hallelujah Chorus'. To be honest, I was really chuffed and walked into the music library to choose my programme and plan the evening's entertainment. There are only two reasons that a band plays at a mess dinner – the loyal toast to the Queen, and the regimental marches. As for the rest, you may as well be playing to yourself, as the officers, or sergeants, whatever the case may be, are usually too pissed to notice and don't really give a damn. This particular dinner night was being held in the Royal Corps of Signals' mess, and as the signals' band was unavailable, we took their place. Being a sergeants' mess dinner, the band's senior ranks took no part and had a night-off, hence my being chosen to conduct that night. The night went well. We would play a couple of pieces, have a fag and a swig of beer, and then play a couple more pieces and repeat the process all over again. This was perfectly possible, as we were in an annex next to the main dining room and out of view of the merry-makers within. The Mess Sergeant poked his head around the door, looked at me and muttered, "Five minutes." I nodded, as my pulse rate started to climb and I told the lads to sit down.

As I said earlier, the only reason that you're there in the first place is to play the loyal toast. Some would say that it's all a bit of a waste of time really and I would agree. But, 'Ours is not to reason why', and 'Just do as you're told, will you?' The whole mess suddenly fell silent, as I lifted up my arm and waited. The tinkle of a small bell rang through the mess and a disembodied voice announced, "Mr Vice, the Queen." After a short pause, another voice, equally disembodied, said, "Gentlemen, the Queen," as the whole mess responded, "The Queen." That was my cue to bring down my arm and for the band to play the first six bars of the national anthem. I breathed a sigh of relief, as the babble of voices recommenced inside the dining room and I realised that I'd got it right.

There's a tradition in the army that whoever conducts a mess night dinner, be he bandmaster, or, as in my case, lowly lance corporal, is invited to the dining room for a glass of port and a cigar after the loyal toast. For the second time that evening, the Mess Sergeant put his head around the door and beckoned to me. I followed him into the magnificent dining room and glanced around at the gleaming, regimental silver and flickering candlelight. The sergeants, resplendent in their scarlet, mess dinner jackets with gold chevrons, sat back and contentedly puffed on their cigars. Following the sergeant, I approached the head of the table and stood to attention in the best military manner. The head of the mess looked, smiled and said, "Good evening, corporal. Please sit down." "Good evening, sir," I said, and sat in the chair provided, as the head of the mess, the RSM, poured me a large glass of ruby-red port. I politely declined the proffered cigar.

David Paul Spencer, Catterick Camp 1973

The chief guest that night was the local brigadier, and therefore my big boss. He looked over at me quizzically, and said, "I see that you're a lance corporal. Isn't it normally the job of a full corporal to conduct the band at these functions?" "Yes, sir," I said, "but the senior corporal preferred to play and I really enjoy conducting." He nodded thoughtfully as I asked the RSM for his permission to play the regimental marches. He agreed, and not wanting to overstay my welcome, I stood, thanked them and left.

"OK, lads," I said, as soon as I got back into the ante-room. We were lucky, as there were only ten different regiments in the mess that night and so we only had ten marches to play – I've known it to be much higher. The sergeants, who were thoroughly well oiled by this time, banged the table with gusto as we played their regimental music to loud cheers and finally left for a few beers and a well-earned supper in the back of the mess.

Two days later, I was promoted to full corporal. And no, I didn't get a bunk!

I must say that Richmond is a nice little town and the gateway to the Yorkshire Dales. One Saturday afternoon, a group of us were sitting in a pub getting quietly drunk and reading the horse-racing form, ready for the next race at York. I finished my pint, stood and headed for the door, saying to anyone who cared to listen, "I'll be back in a minute."

"Are you going to the bookies, Spanner?" asked Joe Wilson, while 'Dob' Davies looked on, owlishly. The pints that he'd already consumed were beginning to take their toll, as he nodded, while a secret little smile played at the corner of his mouth.

"No, I won't be long," I said as I walked out and into the sunlight. I was more than a bit annoyed, two stripes and no bunk. "Fuck you all," I muttered to myself, "It's time to do something about it." I walked into the newsagents and picked up the local newspaper, my mind made up. After I'd paid, I strolled across the town square and headed for another pub. I ordered a pint, sat down and looked in the property to rent section, ignoring the squaddies nosily playing pool over in the corner. "Too expensive," I muttered to myself, as I worked my way down the column. My eye came to rest on a little add somewhere near to the end, "Now that's a possible," I said out loud as I gulped down my pint and left.

"Studio to rent. Available from the first of October." I knew exactly where it was and retracing my steps headed over in the direction of the address given in the ad. Just next to the fish-and-chip shop stood an 'olde worlde café' that sold sausage, egg and chips to the passing tourists. I'd been in there many times to sample the delights of their house speciality, roast beef and Yorkshire pudding. As I walked in, a couple of hikers, a handsome young lad and his girlfriend were just leaving. I couldn't resist looking at the boy encased in tight shorts as they walked out. The owner, a red-haired woman who wore 'Dame Edna' style glasses and answered to the name of Jean, looked over and smiled.

"Hello, love," she said, a cigarette dangling precariously from the corner of her mouth, as a stream of smoke curled up towards the ceiling. Hygiene seemed to be low on the agenda. "Do you want something to eat?"
"No thanks, Jean, not at the moment. It's about this ad," I said, indicating the newspaper.
"Are you interested, then? I didn't think that you were married."
"I'm not, and yes I am." She looked at me, puzzled for a moment, as I continued, "I'm Interested in the studio."
"There's a young squaddie and his wife in there at the moment, but they've just got a married quarter. I can't let you see it until Monday though, it being the weekend."

Her voice trailed off, and she looked at me, the smoke from her cigarette making a halo around her head. "Can I see it on Monday evening, Jean?"

"Course you can, if you want."

A note of pleading entered my voice, as I said, urgently, "Be an angel, Jean, give me first refusal, will you?"

"All right. To be honest I can't see a married couple being interested. It's a bit small. The only reason those two up there took it," she said, vaguely indicating with her finger in the general direction of upstairs, "was because they couldn't find anything else. Newly weds, you know. It'd suit you though."

"Great! Is six o'clock OK?"

"No problem."

"See you then," I said, as I headed towards the door and walked back to the pub, my heart singing as I watched the young hikers climbing aboard the bus to Darlington. I eyed the boy appreciatively, envying the lucky young girl, as I thought to myself, "I'm taking that flat, whether they like it or not." My mind was made up.

"Where have you been?" demanded Dob, drunkenly, eyeing me with suspicion.

"Mind your own business and it's your round," I replied, as the others said nothing, their heads buried in the newspaper looking for the elusive winner.

A look of surprise flashed across Rod Parker's face as I made my request. "You want to live out?" he asked.

"Yes, sir."

"It's a bit unusual, isn't it?" he said, eyeing me, as if wondering what my hidden agenda was. "Very well, I'll talk to the band president and see what he says. I can't make you any promises though."

I nodded and said, "Thank you, sir," and walked out. It must be said that my wanting to live out was something totally unheard of in those days. In fact, I never came across any other single man doing it during my whole army service. I was spurred on by my need for some peace and privacy and to be able to escape for a while. Imagine a typical evening; at one end of the room you have the television blaring away, whilst at the other, a brass band aficionado is listening to the Black Dyke Mills band playing the latest test piece, and you in the middle trying to read a good book. Constantly surrounded by noise and distraction, I often found myself on the verge of screaming and I longed for some solitude.

The positive answer was not long in coming, but I would still have to pay my living and food expenses as if I was still living in the barracks. I didn't care as I jumped with joy and took the bus into Richmond and my meeting with Jean. We climbed the rickety stairs up to the top of the house, as Jean quietly tapped at the door and we both walked in. The room was small, with a double bed in one corner, a large table and two not over-comfortable armchairs that had seen better days. It was in the eaves, with a small skylight set in the sloping roof, and a tiny bathroom off to one side. A very heavily pregnant young girl stood at an ironing board, her light, wispy blond hair awry. She looked like a schoolgirl, and undoubtedly had been, just a few months earlier. She already looked careworn and I imagined what she would be like in ten years time. Her equally young husband was sprawled in one of the armchairs, wearing a figure-hugging pair of jeans and showing his body off to perfection. A copy of the *Sun* newspaper lay at his feet, and his naked upper torso showed a large tattoo of an eagle, the vivid colours of the predator making his skin look unnaturally white. I couldn't keep my eyes off him. He stood up, his boyish face and cropped brown hair making him incredibly attractive. His figure-hugging jeans showed off the contours of his lower body to perfection, almost as if he were nude. "Be careful, David," I warned myself as I quickly averted my eyes, smiled and murmured, "Hello." He just nodded, uninterestedly. I looked around the room and turned to Jean. "I'll take it," I said, my heart filling with joy. To some the place would have been little more than a tip, but to me it was a palace.

The remains of a large fish-and-chip supper lay on the table. I was curled up in one of the battered old armchairs, contentedly looking up at the stars framed in the small aperture above my head, a can of lager held loosely in my right hand. Behind me the lovely sounds of Beethoven's third piano concerto filled the air as I looked around at my new home with satisfaction. It hadn't really sunk in yet. I had privacy and my own private space, luxury beyond imagining. I'd got home from work, just like normal people do, soaked in a hot bath and opened a beer. Taking a long satisfied swig, I pondered on the various merits of Chinese or fish-and-chips, deciding on the easiest option as the fish shop was just next door. Now, a self-satisfied grin all over my face, I lost myself in contemplation as I viewed the long, lazy weekend ahead. "All that I need now, is a nice young partner to share that pit," I thought, as I looked over at the seemingly enormous bed in the corner of the room. "Now, now, David," I admonished myself, "don't start to get greedy. Count your blessings, my boy. It certainly beats that barrack room, with the television blaring in the background," I reflected, as I stood, stretched lazily and started to get undressed.

Jean and I became firm friends and I took most of my meals in the café. I became well-known around the town and soon discovered a local a few minutes walk away, which for some reason was never used by the squaddies – something to be thankful for. My routine became totally ordinary. I would get up, put my uniform on and take the 7.15 bus into the barracks, arriving at about the same time as the married members of the band as they walked in from their various quarters. It became something of a joke, as we all met up and headed towards the band practice room together. I was an honorary married lad.

Jean was not an early riser and would languish in bed until mid-morning, a cup of coffee in one hand and a cigarette in the other. I'd often pop in on my days off, sit on the end of the bed and have a good gossip about anyone and everyone. I think that Jean sussed me out very quickly, but never said anything as she regarded me over the top of her 'Dame Edna' glasses. She was to save me from a lot of very big trouble later on. Those days were relatively happy ones for me, or at least, as happy as they were going to get for the foreseeable future. It was at about this time that a new intake of young musicians arrived fresh from boys' service and one or two of them were very cute indeed. One especially caught my eye, a young man of eighteen, with floppy, light brown hair and the look of 'Lord Alfred Douglas' about him. His name was Felix and I fancied him like mad.

Gay friends have often asked me why I didn't escape onto the gay scene in those years. After all, homosexuality was no longer illegal in England by this time, and as my gay brothers and sisters came out of their various closets, a gay community was beginning to emerge. What stopped me was fear – the fear of discovery. It may seem irrational now, but at the time was very real to me. Whenever I thought of it, and I did from time to time, it was quickly dismissed. I would imagine being caught up in a police raid and handed over to the military police with glee by their civilian counterparts. Denial also played a strong part – I had been having sex with other men for years, but still believed that I was only going through a 'phase' and would soon be normal. So what did I need a gay bar for? Such places were for queers and I wasn't a queer, was I?

Musically, things continued much as they had for the previous years and I still loved it. The number of military tattoos that we did, something that I enjoyed immensely, marks those years. I loved the massed bands and the grand finalé that finished each evening's performance in a blaze of colour, the music echoing all over the stadium. One that particularly comes to mind is the military musical pageant at Wembley Stadium. The finalé, with over one thousand musicians and various cannons, was Tchaikovsky's '1812' overture, conducted by Lieutenant-Colonel Trevor Sharp, one of the big names in military music at that time. The Royal Tournament at Earls Court in London also deserves a mention. This world-famous event, much loved by the public, was an absolute nightmare for the participants. We literally had to live inside Earls Court and it was bedlam. I don't know how many military personnel were living inside the place, but it was a hell of a lot, and you could forget any idea of getting a good night's sleep. We were crammed in there like cattle. Rod Parker said that anyone who wanted to live out could do so. Joe Wilson, myself and two other members of the band took advantage of the situation and moved into the old Union Jack Club. Joe and I shared a room together. I'll give Parker his due – he was very good like that. I remember another occasion when the band arrived to do a concert at a seaside town and our accommodation consisted of a row of camp beds inside a drill hall. Parker said that anybody who wanted to find a hotel was welcome. I did just that, the only one of the band to do so. Christ! I was a fussy old queen, even in those days.

I was becoming more than a little interested in Felix and wondered if I dare do something about it. We had a conversation one day that gave me some encouragement and I believe was purposely engineered by him. We had a sergeant who mysteriously reappeared half way through a tour as an instructor at the depot. No reason was ever given for his reappearance and we all speculated on what had happened. Felix and I were talking and he said that he thought he could throw some light on the subject. He told me that some letters had been found in the possession of a young boy musician, who baby-sat for the sergeant and his wife. It was a known fact that these two had an open marriage and didn't much care what the other got up to. The letters were incriminating, and seemed to indicate that something was going on between the boy and the sergeant. I don't know the truth of any of this, but must admit that if what Felix said was true, I couldn't work out how the sergeant got away with it. In view of what was to happen to me later, I find it all a bit hard to believe. However, the conversation seemed to indicate to me that sweet little Felix might not have been so innocent after all. I cautioned him and told him not to repeat any of what he'd told me. "The one thing that you don't want to do, Felix, is make any enemies. You've still got a long time to serve and so I'd keep it to yourself, if I were you." He nodded, as we looked directly into each other's eyes. I picked up the signal and vowed to do something about it at the first opportunity. Perhaps I could put my little attic to good use.

Rod Parker decided that it would be a good idea if the band were to make a record. This was arranged, and the recording session, planned for a Saturday, was to last all day. We set everything up in the gymnasium and started to record. During a smoke break, I saw my chance and discreetly walked over to Felix. As I approached, he looked up and nodded. We'd been told that the Monday and Tuesday would be off, and I had visions of a weekend of sex with the very desirable Felix. Speaking quietly, so as not to be overheard, I said, casually, "Have you got any plans for the weekend, Felix?"
"No. Have you got any ideas?' he asked, looking at me knowingly.
"How would you like to come over to my place and spend the weekend with me?" My heart was beating rapidly, as I waited for his answer.
"OK, why not. But Dave?"
"Yes?"
"Keep it to yourself, won't you?"
"Of course, don't worry about that," I answered, as I thought quickly. "Listen, I'll meet you at seven in the pub." I chose a pub that none of the band members ever used, and so the chances of the two of us being seen together were slim.
He replied, "All right." As I walked away, erotic images of us both together flashed through my mind.

Jumping out of the bath, I quickly got dressed and headed towards the pub and my meeting with Felix. It was quiet as I ordered a pint and whisky chaser and sat down, looking from time to time towards the door and hoping that no one else from the band would walk in. Felix arrived just after seven, bought himself a pint and joined me. We decided that it wasn't a good idea for us to hang around. With that in mind, I'd already stocked up with cans of lager and a supply of whisky after the recording session. We finished our drinks and left, heading across the square and up to my flat. As we walked in we smiled at each and started to relax. I poured us both a drink and we sat facing each other, not speaking for a moment. Lying back in the chair, I draped my leg over one of the arms, my excitement obvious. Felix looked at me carefully and I wondered if I'd made a dreadful mistake. I needn't have bothered. He started to tell me in graphic detail about the wild sex that he'd had one dark night with his brother's friend, in the back of a car. His story was incredibly erotic and we were soon rolling all over the bed together, our naked bodies entwined and covered in sweat.

I awoke first the next morning, with a massive hangover and my old friend, guilt, staring me in the face. Instead of lying together and talking, as lovers should do, I couldn't wait to get out. Before he'd barely opened his eyes, I was up and dressed. I quickly left, muttering something about getting the Sunday papers. I didn't hurry myself and when I got back, Felix, to my eternal regret, had left. Why did I do this to myself? Felix was in bed making love with me because he wanted to be. Why couldn't I accept that and enjoy it. Why did this demon called guilt haunt me? I spent the rest of the weekend getting pissed. When I saw him on the Tuesday morning, he refused to look me in the eye, and I don't blame him. I think that Felix from that day on regarded me with both contempt and loathing. I know that I felt nothing but contempt and loathing for myself.

Richmond was shrouded in darkness, the streets deserted and silent, as I glanced at the luminous dial of my watch. It read 4.00 am. There was a faint odour of stale fish-and-chips lingering in the air from the previous night's fry-up, making me feel slightly nauseous. I turned and glanced up, looking towards the roof and my little haven in the sky, scene of so much activity only a few short hours previously. The night before, I had gone to my local with the intention of getting drunk, and at the same time got lucky. It was almost as if someone had looked down at me and said, "OK, Dave, this might be the last time that you ever have it, so I'll be kind to you." And kind he was.

I'd noticed a very attractive young man, very small in stature, but very well put together. We started talking and it turned out that he was a trainee jockey from one of the local riding stables. We talked and drank together for the whole evening, both knowing that we were going to end up in bed together. As closing time approached, we finished our drinks and headed back to my place. We had great sex together, and he finally left at about 2.00 am, at the same time that my married colleagues would be saying their fond and very passionate farewells to their wives. I reasoned that as that option wasn't open to me, thank God, I would say my own goodbyes to the handsome young jockey instead. I'd dozed on the top of the bed, to be abruptly awakened by the raucous call of the alarm. Why fond farewells? We were all off to fight in a bloody and dangerous war.

I lit a cigarette and inhaled deeply, shivering in the cold October air. My camouflaged infantry combat kit felt strange and alien. As I hadn't worn it for years, that wasn't really surprising. I heard the car approaching, and as it screeched to a halt Bob stuck his head out of the window. "Are you ready, Dave?" he asked, looking at me. "As ready as I'm ever going to fucking well be," I answered as I threw my suitcase into the boot and jumped into the passenger seat.

The City of Belfast loomed out of the mist and rain. Its lights twinkled in the pre-dawn darkness, giving an air of both menace and depression as if saying, "Keep out. You're not welcome here." The ferry slowly inched its way towards the jetty as thick ropes sailed through the air and were caught and made fast by the hands waiting below. We disembarked quickly and ran towards the waiting three-ton trucks, the tailgates already lowered and ready for us. Driving out of the city at speed we headed towards Hollywood and Palace Barracks, home to the respected (at least by us) 3rd Battalion of the Parachute Regiment and our home for the next four months. The Paras, as they're known, are amongst the toughest and best-trained soldiers in the world.

"Drop your kit and get straight down to the armoury," shouted Bob Shaw, as we looked around at our new home with dismay. It was a long, prefabricated hut, with a concrete floor and no visible means of heating. Stretching down each wall was a line of double bunks. It reminded me of just about every prisoner-of-war film that I'd ever seen.

I was handed a self-loading rifle, a magazine and ten rounds of ammunition, and along with the other lads headed back to the trucks. It wasn't yet dawn as we clambered back on board, this time separated into teams of two men for each vehicle. We loaded the unfamiliar and deadly weapons, shoving the magazine into place, as the lorries screeched away with a sense of urgency. This was to be our first job – escort to the departing regiment that we had been sent out to relieve. I sat on the back of the lorry, the muzzle of my weapon pointing upwards, as a swarm of squaddies jumped up and rapidly filled the back of the lorry. "Come on, let's get the fuck out of here," shouted one of the men. "Christ! I'm going to give my misuss a right banging tonight and then I'm going to get legless," said another, loudly. The engines revved up and pulled out onto the roadway, heading at speed back towards the docks.

A huge squaddie sitting next to me said, "All right, Corp? Have you got one up the spout?" I was puzzled for a moment, until it dawned on me that he was asking whether I had got a round of ammunition in the chamber of the weapon (against regulations). I said "No". "I would if I were you. Stuff the

124

regulations," he said sagely, as we pulled up by the side of the ferry and they all jumped off with whoops of joy, their four month stint at an end. As he was leaving, my squaddie friend said, "Good luck, Corp. Keep your fucking head down, or those bastards will blow it off." He gave me a wave and headed at a jog towards the waiting vessel. "So this was Northern Ireland," I thought to myself, as I watched his rapidly departing back. My flack jacket was already beginning to feel heavy and uncomfortable.

Compared to the life of the real soldiers in the regiment, ours was relatively simple, but not without its dangers. Belfast was a dangerous place and the IRA were not about to differentiate between a squaddie and a member of the regimental band. As we weren't trained combat soldiers, we were kept away from foot patrols or house-to-house searches, as our involvement in any action of that nature would have put everyone in grave danger. The CO was no fool and knew our limitations. We could, however, be useful and do our bit. It's interesting to note that after this tour we were one of the first bands in the army to do full medical training, something that every army musician does today. Army musicians have served as medics with distinction in just about every conflict since then, including the Falklands and both Gulf wars.

The new CO had taken over the regiment on our return from Berlin and was determined that the band would be with the regiment during the Northern Ireland tour. I disliked him, to be honest. However, he was a very fine soldier and well loved by his men. He led from the front, and as a soldier I have respect and admiration for him, a brave man.

One morning we were awoken in the early hours and told to get dressed. It was bitterly cold as we made our way to the notorious Crumlin Road Goal and relieved the guard there. This was during the time of 'Internment without Trial', instituted by the then government. The battalion was taking part in a massive operation against the IRA and every man was needed. This grim Victorian pile was a place that I got to know well over those months, and we were often on the receiving end of a torrent of foul-mouthed abuse from the wives of the internees. On this particular night, at about 3.00 am, we mounted the watchtowers that were spaced around the walls. These brick and concrete fortresses only had slits for looking out of and the steel door downstairs was firmly locked. There were two men to each tower and on this occasion the CSM suggested that as those bastards were keeping us up we should turn on the searchlights. This we did, straight into the prisoners' cells. I'm not sure that this action was strictly legal. All hell broke loose as the prisoners woke up and started to riot. The sound of tin mugs being angrily smashed against the bars of the cells echoed around the prison, while shouts of "English bastards" could be heard from the prisoners. It was a place filled with hate. An angry phone call from the chief prison officer followed and we turned off the lights – shortly afterwards things started to settle down.

Escort and guard duties were our lot during those months and fatigue was an ever-constant enemy. Escorts were quite dangerous, as you were exposed and vulnerable to sniper fire. In those days, the soldiers stood on the back of an open *Land Rover*, one facing forward, the other back. There were two *Land Rovers* like this, one at the front and one at the back, with the vehicle being escorted in the middle. It was no picnic, driving at high speed down the road in the early hours of an icy cold December morning.

There's one story that I'd rather not tell, but not to do so would be breaking the rules that I've set myself. On Christmas Eve, a group of us had been drinking in the NAAFI in Palace Barracks. The official rule was no more than two beers per man, but this was easily overcome, and we were all quite drunk. Graham was a lad that I'd been pursuing for a long time. I knew that I had him, when on a visit to London, after I'd been chatting him up all evening, he asked me to kiss him, which I gladly did. We'd left the pub and found a darkened alleyway and proceeded to have a long, lingering snog. We both took a huge risk that night. Of course, we couldn't take things any further and returned to barracks. Anyway, this evening in the barracks, Graham suggested that we find somewhere quiet. Believe it or not, I was hesitant as it didn't seem appropriate somehow. But I quickly gave in when I saw how keen he was, and anyway I was feeling randy. We found a bathroom in a darkened wash house and got on with it, leaving quietly afterwards.

The next day, as we were sitting down to the usual turkey and trimmings, I heard my name called. I looked up and saw a colour sergeant I knew well looking over towards and gesturing for me to go over to him. As I approached, he looked at me and said quietly, "I've got something that belongs to you." I was surprised as he handed me my army identity card, and continued, "I know what you were doing last night. I suggest that you be careful in future. The next time, you may not be so lucky."

I firmly believe that he and I belonged to the same club, and that's what saved me. If it had been anyone else... I nodded and quietly thanked him. I had been let off the hook; how much longer could my luck last?

Eventually our tour was over and we landed back in Blighty. True to form, on the troop train heading back towards Catterick, Rod Parker said that anyone wishing to go directly home on leave could do so. I asked one of the lads to hand my weapon in for me and did just that, still dressed in my combat gear. When I walked in, there was no one at home. I walked upstairs, undressed, fell into bed and slept around the clock.

On the rare occasions that I wear my General Service Medal, I wear it with pride.

After our return from Northern Ireland, things quickly returned to normal, our experiences in that troubled land soon pushed to the back of our minds. Most evenings you would find me propping up the bar in my local watering hole in Richmond. Over the months, I had become popular with the locals. One night, a woman I knew very well came into the lounge accompanied by a delightful young man who I'd never seen before. The woman was a very good friend of Jean, something that was to get me out of a lot of serious trouble later. The boy, Mark, was her son and about seventeen, with dark wavy hair, brown eyes and the most engaging smile. I became totally besotted by him and he soon became the object of my sexual fantasies. Like a lovesick boy, I'd rush home from the barracks, get ready and head for the pub, in the hope of seeing him. We became good friends, he, of course, having no inkling of my inner most feelings towards him. Over the years I've learned two things – firstly, that you cannot make somebody gay, no matter how much you may wish it; and secondly, that you should never, ever make a mess on your own doorstep. I quickly forgot both rules.

One Saturday evening I was sitting in my usual corner, when mother and son came in. We had a nice evening, talking and laughing, while I eyed the beautiful Mark, appreciatively. At closing time, Mark's mother invited me around for a night cap, an offer that I quickly accepted. I'd had enough to drink that night and the whisky that she offered slightly tipped me over the edge. After a while, and after glancing at her watch a few times, she announced that she was going to bed. I had over-stayed my welcome, but didn't give a damn, just as long as I could continue to feast my eyes on the object of my desires for just a little longer. After she'd left, I did the most stupid thing imaginable and came on to him strongly, making it quite clear what I had in mind. The poor boy was horrified, his face turning red with embarrassment. Realising my mistake, I apologised and quickly left, scuttling like a thief into the night. Unknown to me, his mother had been standing behind the door, listening to every word that I uttered.

I had just got back from the barracks on the Monday evening when there was a knock at the door and Jean walked in. I'd never seen her look so serious, as she said, "What were you up to on Saturday night, Dave?" Before I could reply, she continued, "I had a visit from my friend this morning, and she was incandescent with rage. You bloody fool. It took me all of my time to persuade her not to go to the police. It was a good job that you didn't lay a finger on Mark. If you had, there would have been nothing that I could do for you. As it is, she's promised to let the matter drop. But for Christ's sake, don't you dare go near to that boy again. I told her that it really didn't mean anything and that you were drunk."

I slumped into the armchair, my face turning white with fear, as my mind went back to Brian all of those years previously and his involvement with a minor. My hands shook, as I lit a cigarette and inhaled, deeply. "I'm sorry, Jean. What a fucking idiotic thing to do," I said, realising what a lucky escape that I'd had and it was all thanks to Jean.

"Listen, love," she said kindly, "I've often suspected that you were that way, but this is a small place and people talk. If I were you, I'd go looking in Darlington or somewhere like that if you want a bloke."

I couldn't help but smile bitterly, realising the truth of what she'd just said, but still not prepared to admit that what I really needed was the company of like-minded people. After she left, I poured a scotch and sat down, staring in to space as the room darkened around me. I was skating on very thin ice and the cracks were getting ever bigger. I realised that if I wasn't very careful I'd fall through and find myself in very deep water indeed.

Oh how we fool ourselves. That night I walked into the pub. How could I have imagined that she'd say nothing to anyone? If I'd been a Jew wearing the Star of David on my breast in Nazi Germany, my reception couldn't have been more glacial.

The room fell silent, as I looked around at the faces of my 'friends' now cold and full of hate. "Queer," some one muttered, as I turned and walked back out of the door, realising that my position was now untenable.

Shortly after the Mark incident, fate was again to take a hand in the management of my affairs. One morning, Parker called me into his office and asked me if I'd be prepared to go down to the depot as an instructor. I say 'asked'. I've often wondered what he'd have said, had I refused, but I was being offered a way out. My little house in the sky had now lost all meaning as a place of refuge, and anyway it couldn't have lasted forever. It quickly occurred to me that my time in the army would come to an end during my two years there, and I suspect that this was something not lost on Parker either. I agreed, as he smiled and told me that I'd spend the summer with the band and leave at the beginning of September.

As I was leaving, he said to me, "I'm sending you down to the depot, Corporal Spencer, even though I think that you have a drink problem." At that moment I despised the man. If I had a drink problem, then so did ninety percent of the band, including him. I just couldn't let it go, as I turned around and said quietly, "A drink problem, Sir? Have I ever been so drunk that I've turned my car over?" (Peter had done just that, a few months previously.) "Have I been so drunk that I've smashed up a valuable instrument and got away with it?" (Peter again.) "Have I ever been so drunk that I was incapable of doing my job?" He looked at me and said nothing, as I seethed with the injustice of his words and walked out, closing the door quietly behind me. "You low bastard!" I thought to myself. Rarely have I felt such rage. "If I do have a problem, it's not so much drink, but mean-minded people like you, with the mindset of Nazis." It was that conversation that triggered off my intense dislike of 'holier-than-thou' bigots who have the audacity to think that they can treat me and people like me as something unwholesome. The word *'Untermensch'* comes to mind. The mindset of these people is no better than that of those men who were responsible for the deaths of millions because they judged them to be different. Today, if I can, I always treat such people and their attitudes with contempt. Usually, like most cowards, they back down.

During my time in Catterick, I often spent my leave time with a very dear and elderly aunt in Worthing. Fannie, my father's sister, would have been more at home living in a past era. She was a genteel lady who would never leave home without wearing her gloves, maintaining that no woman of breeding should be seen out of doors without them; a petite woman and a dreadful chatterbox who would talk endlessly, due to the fact that she was very lonely. We gave each other mutual support and I can never repay her many kindnesses to me.

My father's family was very well-to-do, unlike my mother's. Their father owned a basket making business in the Aston district of Birmingham. The family had been basket makers for generations, and while not rich, they enjoyed a comfortable standard of living. Fannie was a spinster and lived alone in a small flat in an old Victorian house, shared with some very eccentric characters indeed. Rosy, a faded actress type, who drank an enormous amount of sherry each day, lived on the same floor. I would go in each afternoon and have a tipple with her, from 3.00 until 4.00. As the hour passed and she got more drunk, her wig would become more and more awry.

On the ground floor lived a brother and sister – the brother, John, always dressed in regimental blazer and tie, the front of the blazer usually being covered in a fine layer of cigarette ash. With a thin moustache and thick rimmed spectacles, he both looked and sounded like 'Colonel Blimp'. There was one other occupant, a divorced man called Bob, who affected friendship towards me but was anything but. Unknown to him, I once overheard him remark to Rosy that I "wasn't like a real man at all." I also had no illusions about Rosy, so from time to time I'd descend on this bunch of misfits and blend in quite nicely.

131

Every evening, Fan and I would go off to a concert at the end of the pier. The musicians were very good indeed and they had a large and very varied repertoire. Their number varied, with anything from three players to a large salon orchestra. I spent very many happy hours with Fan and know that she was very glad of my company. She was extremely generous and shared everything with me, something that I'll never forget. I never had much money in those days and sadly, when I was in a position to be more generous, she was dead.

The lack of mention of women in these pages may not be suprising, given the circumstances. However, like many gay men of my generation, I often used women as a smoke-screen, something that is still quite common today. This is not something I am proud of, but I can think of at least four occasions when I could be seen walking hand-in-hand with some young woman, totally false, an insult to them, and usually not fooling anyone. Many years later Peter pointed my behaviour out to me and told me that Darren had done exactly the same thing before he came out as gay. Peter told me that he felt that there was something not quite right, just a feeling that something didn't fit. He was to remember that feeling whenever he saw Darren in exactly the same situation.

I don't look back at those times with any pride. There was one poor girl in Belfast who very bravely came to weekly dances held at Palace Barracks and who liked me enormously. To my great shame, I courted her assiduously and led her on, even talking of possible engagement. The night before we left Belfast I swore undying love to her and then promptly forgot her as soon as we had landed back in England. I'll never forgive myself for my behaviour towards those innocent young women, who I used as pawns. The only thing I can say in my defence is that I was so scared of being caught out that I would have done anything to avoid it. The irony of it all is that I now know that I was fooling no one, except myself. I can only say this – I hope with all my heart that those women found husbands and went on to live happily married lives. One thing is certain – they wouldn't have found it with me!

Towards the end of a two-week leave, I started to feel very ill indeed, and I had dreadful pain around the stomach area I was forced to see a doctor, who must have been eighty if he was a day. It was obvious to me, when he discovered that I was a soldier, that he thought I was swinging the lead. He gave me some kind of stomach powder and a certificate for a week off. Army regulations are very strict for a soldier who goes sick whilst on leave. Any certificate sent in must have 'Unfit to travel' written on it. Mine didn't. I was fully aware of the rules, but to be honest, I felt so ill that I ignored them. I'm very surprised that the military police didn't come looking for me. In hindsight, I should have gone to the A & E department of the nearest hospital. The train journey back to Catterick was an absolute nightmare and I dragged myself into barracks the following morning, more dead than alive. Bob Shaw, who was then the band sergeant, wasn't best pleased to see me, and threatened that I would be charged with being absent without leave, which technically I was. How I refrained from telling him where to go, thus making things worse, I don't know.

The regiment were away somewhere and I reported to the medical centre in the barracks next door. The MO, a Lieutenant-Colonel, took one look at me and said, "Christ, Corporal, you're as yellow as a dog." He turned and called for the orderly and told him to take a urine sample. As soon as he saw the results, he called for an ambulance and I was whisked off to the British military hospital.

On arrival I was put into an isolation ward and told that I had infectious hepatitis. Apparently I was highly infectious and could have no contact with anyone. I even had my own exclusive bedpan, with my name boldly inscribed on it. Parker was really annoyed, as he'd hoped to have me on the summer tour. That was now impossible as my stay in the hospital was to be a long one.

One sunlit morning, I was standing in the hospital grounds dressed in pyjamas and dressing gown. As I looked over towards the main road, I saw the band coach go whizzing past. I lifted my hand and waved. Whether anyone saw me or not I don't know, but nobody returned my wave.

My stay in the hospital was one long, pleasant holiday. My brother, mother and father visited me and Uncle Walter and Aunt Elsie came over from Leeds. The medical board medically downgraded me for one year and I was off the booze for six months. It's ironic that I've since discovered that I've never had hepatitis in my life. Whenever I mentioned to my doctors here in Luxembourg that I once had hepatitis, after doing a blood test, they've never been able to trace any sign of it. One thing is sure, there was certainly something very wrong with me all of those years ago. Could it be that it was the first sign of my present illness?

There's one more highly amusing story to tell. One day, the hospital's RSM came to see me and told me that I'd been charged with absence without leave and had to appear before the company commander the next morning. He solemnly told me, trying hard not to laugh, that an ambulance would pick me up the next morning to take me into the barracks to answer the charges. My doctor, a captain, also highly amused, came to see me and told me not to forget to tell them that I was still highly infectious. It was obvious to me that the doctor had already spoken with the OC and put him in the picture, but army justice had to be seen to be done. I duly arrived and approached the CSM who eyed me warily as I warned him of my highly infectious state. It was hat and belt off time again, but with a difference. In deference to my delicate condition, I marched in, in normal time, rather than quick time. I was given a bollicking for not following the correct procedure for sickness while on leave, and the case was dismissed. On the way back to the hospital the army

134

ambulance driver and myself were rolling around with laughter at the absurdity of it all.

I was finally discharged and sent on two weeks' sick leave. Before I went, I returned to an empty barracks, packed all of my kit and left Catterick behind, never to return, and without the slightest regret. The final act of the play was about to start, and, for me, the worst period of my life.

Deluge

I say the worst period of my life. In the beginning, nothing could have been further from the truth. In fact, my early days at Bassingbourne were probably the happiest of my whole army career, which was the one thing that lulled me into a false sense of security, making me think that perhaps things weren't so bad after all. The problem of my sexuality seemed to fade and I pushed it to the back of my mind. It was as if by moving to somewhere new, I could somehow wipe the slate clean and start all over again. How could I have been so stupid? My denial was as strong as ever and I still refused to face the facts about myself. I closed my mind and put my head back into the sand. There's always an 'if' in the equation, isn't there? If only I'd have seen my time out and gone, like any sensible person would have done, but no, I was going to have to learn the hard way.

The instructors had a great deal of power, power that could very easily be abused and often was. However, in my supreme arrogance I thought myself above such things and would never abuse my position, would I? In the end, my betrayal of trust would be far greater than anyone's and would lead to my downfall. I had been heading towards it for years and was lucky that I'd got away with it for so long. In the end I'd force myself to fall on my sword and, in an obscure way, do the right thing. I'd gone a complete cycle in my army service, from boy soldier to being an instructor of boy soldiers. I lived with these soldiers and spent hours helping and talking with them – my door was never closed. They liked and respected me. I was firm but fair, never allowing anyone to step out of line, but at the same time handling them all with a certain amount of humour and tolerance. They ranged in age from 16 to 18, and most were excellent musicians. The standard of musicianship had certainly gone up since my own boys' service days. But they were still boys and I had the care of them.

For example, one of the lads would come to my bunk in the evening and collect my kit. He was a nice boy, a Londoner, always laughing and joking. He'd knock on my door and hold out his hand, a cheeky grin across his face, as I handed him my shoes and trousers to be cleaned ready for the next morning. At the same time, I'd hand him some money. I don't remember how much, but a fair amount. Many NCO's would have coerced someone into doing the job and saved themselves some money. I couldn't do that and was both popular and respected as a result. They were lovely lads in more ways than one, but it was an inviolate rule of my own that I would never cross that particular line.

I did a lot of conducting. I had my own brass quartet whose musicianship brought them second prize in a competition in the north of England. The brass band world is very competitive and jealousies abound. On the night of the competition, someone laid a complaint against us with the judges, claiming that my boys were professionals, a claim that I was swift to deny, as the boys were still under training. It was a mean-spirited action and was quickly overruled by the judges. Their performance that night was sparkling. The piece, an overture by Weber, finished in a glistening cascade of notes to great applause. That night, I was offered a job of taking over as permanent conductor of a very fine band. As I have already mentioned, I was later invited to conduct the premier of a piece for children's choir and orchestra, a performance that made the local newspapers. Life looked good for me, and a third stripe seemed to be a distinct possibility, as my superiors thought highly of me. I would often cycle past the CO and we'd salute each other, passing by with a cheery good morning. This was the man who, a short time later, was going to crucify me if he could. The hubris of it all was to end in a Greek tragedy of momentous proportions.

My life was so rosy that I decided that another three years in the army wouldn't be a bad idea at all. In reality, it was to prove the worst mistake of my life and was to cause me a great deal of unnecessary heartache. One fine morning I went and saw my boss. The director of music was a very nice man called Don Price. He was a captain and we both got on well. I knocked on his door, saluted and said, "Good morning, sir."
"Good morning, Corporal Spencer. What can I do for you?" he asked.
"Well, sir, it's like this. As you know, I'm due to leave the army during my time here." He nodded, as I continued, "Well sir, I've been thinking of signing on again for three more years."
"Go on," he said.
"May I ask, if I signed on again," I hesitated, and then continued, "Could I spend an extra two years here at Bassingbourne?"
"I don't see why not." he replied. "Usually people can't wait to get away from here and return to their bands. Leave it with me and I'll see what I can do."

I smiled, thanked him, saluted and left. It's true that most people go to the depot reluctantly and replacements are hard to find. This is the way that it used to be, although I can't speak for today, as I'm many years out of touch with the modern army. If I was prepared to stay for an extra two years, that would take the pressure off him to find a replacement for me. Anyway, the answer was yes. I'd give them an extra three years and in return I could stay at the depot. I did have an ulterior motive, the possibility of a third stripe. I also reasoned that with the extra two years at the depot, even if I had to return to the band, it would only be for one year before I'd be due for discharge again.

139

There was another reason. I had been in the army since I was 15 years old, so what on earth was I to do in Civvy Street? Oh how quickly we forget. What's the saying? 'Those who forget the lessons of history are doomed to repeat them.' How quickly I forgot my own lessons. I felt great the day that I signed that piece of paper, giving the army another three years of my life.

I was close to a boy called Ian. He would often come into my bunk in the evenings and at weekends. At one time he spent hours cataloguing my extensive record collection, noting everything down in a book. He was due to go down to the school of music and then on to my band. I gave him hints about myself from time to time, which he didn't seem to mind, but was quick to point out that one day he wanted to marry and have children. His message to me was unambiguous. Anyway, at that point I had no intention of breaking my rule and nothing more was said, although our closeness had been duly noted and an attempt would be made to make something out of it at a later date.

Often the boys would be sent off to do certain things and I would usually go too. The other instructors were all married and had no desire to remove themselves from hearth and home. I was delighted to go, as it was always a few days holiday for me, with little to do except keep my eye on them. The last time I rejoined my regiment, a group of the boys all destined for the second battalion of fusiliers and myself went with the regiment to France. The occasion was the 30th anniversary of the D-Day landings in Normandy. The second battalion had once been the Royal Warwickshire Regiment and had landed with the allies on the sixth of June 1944, hence our involvement.

We took no actual part, but were there as observers. For me, it was one of the most moving experiences of my life and I've never forgotten it. Two things stand out in my mind above all others. A small group of French First World War veterans slowly marched past, by now old men, but still proud and upright. I called my party to attention, remembering the sacrifice that my own grandfather had made all those years previously and saluted them out of respect.

Press photo taken onboard an Army troop ship on the way to The 30th Anniversary of the Normandy landings 1975 Corporal Dave Spencer with two Fusiliers

Later that day I noticed a very senior officer, wearing the red beret of the Parachute Regiment heading towards my party. I called the group to attention, turned and saluted. The general returned my salute, shook my hand and introduced himself. My eyes strayed to the array of medals that gleamed from the left breast of his uniform jacket, making my own GSM look like very small beer indeed. I found myself in the presence of the legendary Lieutenant-General Frederick 'Boy' Browning KCVO KBE CB DESO of Arnhem fame. It was he who turned to Montgomery of Alamein prior to the battle and said, "I think we might be going a bridge too far." This prophetic statement has echoed down the years and become part of military history. The one thing I'll always remember about him was his quiet unassuming manner, and yet he was the kind of soldier who would ask his men to follow him through the gates of hell, and they gladly would. He smiled and we conversed together for a while as I introduced the boys from my group. I was proud to have met such an extraordinary man and will never forget his quiet modesty and humour.

Although I didn't know it at the time, it was the last occasion that I would ever be with my regiment. I've never returned. Sadly, if I did, I doubt that I'd be welcome.

There was, for me, one last outing with the boys. We'd entered a team for an army junior tennis tournament, and I took them down to Colchester. As I was a senior NCO, I was of course entitled to my own bunk; however, due to lack of space I mucked in with the lads. It was a large room, with an alcove and two beds leading off it, giving some privacy to the two occupants. Spotting it, I walked over to take possession of one of the beds. When I walked in, I found a lad called Alex, already installed. Believe me, Alex hadn't escaped my notice. Short in stature and slim, with blond hair, blue eyes and an engaging cockney accent, he was almost 18 and would shortly be leaving to join his band. As I entered he smiled knowingly and looked me straight in the eyes, as if saying, "Here you are Corp, a place for just the two of us." God, I must have been very naïve in those days, and turned pink under his gaze. More gruffly than I intended, I said, "What are you doing in here... ? You'll have to move, junior Lance-Corporal Phillips will share this place with me." He shrugged and picked up his kit, giving a little smirk as he walked away. It was almost as if he knew that one day, sooner or later, something would happen between us. Alex had sussed me out and knew exactly what I liked. He'd been there before on many occasions and I assume enjoyed every minute of it. I wasn't being nasty towards him when I told him to move, but as there was a junior NCO in the party he was entitled to the best spot.

Alarm bells should have started ringing loudly in my ears that day. Perhaps they were, but I chose to ignore them.

Alex haunted me, his ghostly presence taunting, saying, "Come on, you know that you want me. I'm game, how about it? Let me teach you a few tricks." One night, I slept with him.

Alex was my nemesis. No blame should be attached to him. The fault is mine alone. It's hard to say who seduced who that night and it's true to say that he was no novice. That night he taught me things that I didn't think possible. But that's no excuse. I didn't possess enough moral fibre to ignore his siren call and caved in to him. The next day, he smiled at me as if nothing had happened between us. I, on the other hand, was devastated at my betrayal of trust and couldn't live with it. Alex was a poisoned chalice and I'd taken a fatal drink.

For years I've played psychiatrist with myself, going over and over the events that followed. It came to me one evening very recently. The answer to the question that I'd been asking myself for over thirty years hit me in the face and was finally answered. Why did I behave in the way I did next? Was it an act of complete madness on my part or was it an act of desperation? I was almost literally about to commit a form of suicide and destroy myself in the most brutal fashion. Everything that I'd achieved was about to go down the pan. Is that why I did it? I think so – after all, it would have been very easy for me to shrug my shoulders and say what a great night I'd had. Alex had been more than up for it, hadn't he? He wasn't about to tell anyone that he had slept with Corporal Spencer, although many men would have done that.

If only life were that simple. Deep within my innermost being, I had crossed a kind of psychological line that I had drawn in the sand, and I could not deny the truth about myself any longer. Now, all these years later, I have a perverse kind of pride that I was able to do what I considered to be the right thing. Whether I liked it or not, it was time to put the years of

143

denial behind me and face up to the truth once and for all. This has been the most difficult part of the book to write, as trying to put a feeling into words is very hard indeed.

I have a good friend, who also happens to be a distinguished psychiatrist, who perhaps explained it far better than I ever could when he said, "David, you'd come to a point in your life when your sub-conscious mind rebelled and said, 'Stop, enough! It's time to stop destroying yourself – if you continue like this there'll be no future for you.'" Although that may sound a little melodramatic, I believe it is no more than the truth.

The night after my sexual encounter with Alex, I was forced at long last to face up to myself. I couldn't deny the evidence any longer and subconsciously at least, decided that I had to do something about it. It wasn't a conscious act on my part; I doubt that I'm that brave.

There was a new recruit, a clarinet player who was doing his basic training. He was an adult soldier of about nineteen. One evening, as I was giving him a clarinet lesson, I coldly and deliberately came on to him, knowing what the result would be – hence why I insisted at the beginning of this book that I had inflicted a gaping, self-inflicted wound on myself. The next morning I reported sick, complaining of problems with my liver. I was put into the camp hospital, and lying in my bed all alone I waited for the axe to fall. It wasn't long in coming.

Unknown to me, the SIB had already been called in, as the soldier had reported me straight away the next day. I now realise that this is exactly what I wanted him to do. That night, I was lying in my hospital bed feeling apprehensive, but strangely calm, when a young recruit came in to my room.
"Hello, Corp," he said cheerily, "I'm going over to the NAAFI and the medical orderly sent me to see if there was anything that you want?"
I smiled, and said, "You could get me a *Mars* bar."

"Yeh, will do," he said as he breezily left my room.

I'd stopped smoking a few months before this incident and was quite proud of myself as a result.

When the lad came back, as he handed me a packet of cigarettes and a box of matches he sheepishly said, "The orderly thought that these would be better, Corp." He hurriedly left, before I could say anything. I looked at the cigarettes and opened the packet, thinking to myself as I lit up and took a huge drag, "Yes, given the circumstances, they probably are better."

Later that evening, the Band Sergeant Major walked in and I knew that my ordeal was about to begin. He looked at me, coldly, distain written all over his face. I was a pariah and no longer worthy of any kindness. "Corporal Spencer," he announced – a few days previously, it'd been Dave. "I Want your keys. All of your keys, your bunk and lockers, everything." "Yes sir," I said, and handed them over. He said nothing as he took them and walked out. The next morning, I left the hospital and headed towards the guardroom, where two members of the special investigation branch were waiting to interview me. The two gentlemen were quiet and polite, but relentless in their interrogation. I admitted nothing more than they already knew. Yes, I had chatted up the new recruit and I didn't really know why. No, I'd never had homosexual relations before and, yes, I did like girls. The interview lasted for about an hour. They were frustrated; I could tell. But I wasn't about to make their life easy and admit to anything more. They finally let me go and I headed towards the CO's office and my fateful meeting with him.

This was the beginning of the worst few months of my life. I put myself under virtual house arrest, only leaving my room when it was absolutely necessary. I lived on sandwiches, alcohol and cigarettes. I avoided contact with other people, fearing their scorn and distain, and scurried around like a hunted rat, preferably at night. I would have been better off in a cell in the guardroom. For hours I paced up and down my room, smoking endless cigarettes and drinking myself into a stupor. They gave me a job in an office pushing around paper clips. Everyday, I expected to be picked up and taken off to await court marshal, and so it dragged on, day in and day out. There was one decision that I had to make and it was impossible for me to put it off any longer. My parents – I had no choice but to tell them. If I was going to end up in a military prison for a few years, it was impossible to keep it from them, and they had to be told. I went to see my boss, whose office was just next to mine. He was a major and was very decent towards me. He immediately agreed when I requested a weekend leave. I left the camp on a Friday afternoon and, full of apprehension at the ordeal ahead, caught the train to London.

Before meeting my parents I tried to get drunk, I mean absolutely legless, but was unable to succeed. When I arrived in Redditch late that Friday night, after getting through the best part of a bottle of whisky, my hands were trembling as I inserted the key and walked into the hallway. My parents weren't expecting me and looked up as I walked in. Dad half stood up when he saw me, and a look of concern flashed across his face. I must have looked dreadful, my expression white, drawn and haggard. My father was nearing seventy at that time, no longer a young man, and I had to tell him that I was a queer. For a man of his generation, my story couldn't have been more shocking, as I sat there and quietly told them my news. My mother's hand hovered over her mouth, while my father looked at me saying nothing. After I'd finished, there was complete silence in the room as I looked from one to the other, feeling strangely calm, now that it was all over.

Dad's acceptance of the situation shows what kind of a man he was. Thoughtful and generous of spirit, he showed great humanity that night, when he said, quietly, "Dave, I don't care what you are. You're my son and that's all that matters." My mother sat through all of this saying nothing, realising that

146

this was something between a father and his son and she should keep her peace, for once. After that weekend, I returned to Bassingbourne and waited.

My next port of call was Queen Alexandra's military hospital at Millbank, London, and a visit to the psychiatrist. Colonel 'L' sat facing me, the red tabs on his collar standing out vividly, and as he told me to sit down he looked closely at me over the top of his half-moon spectacles. "Tell me about yourself, Corporal Spencer," he said quietly. I was cautious, not trusting him. As with the SIB, I wasn't prepared to give anything away and said as little as possible, only telling him the bare minimum about myself. He was wearing a uniform that I'd started to distrust and it didn't matter to me that he was a doctor. I'd become crafty and was beginning to regard anyone who wore khaki uniform as my enemy. There was no way that I was about to admit that I'd being having regular gay sex since my early teens, for fear that my admission would get back to the SIB.

He listened to what I had to say, all the time making notes and nodding occasionally. Finally, he looked up and studied me closely, before giving his verdict. "Corporal Spencer," he said, "I don't believe that you are a homosexual. You're certainly sexually immature, but homosexual, definitely not. I'm going to recommend that you're discharged and then you can start leading a normal life."

I didn't know whether to laugh or cry at the absurdity of it all. For the first time in my life, I was prepared to face up to myself and admit that I was gay and here was this 'expert' telling me that I wasn't. Bullshit! I thought to myself, as I said quietly, "Yes, sir. Thank you, sir." He nodded and looked at me, before continuing, "And stop drinking. Nobody likes a drunk. I'll give you some tablets to help you and I'll send my report to your medical officer."

I walked out of that office in a daze, unable to believe what had just happened. The one certain thing in the world was my sexuality, but I'd been offered a way out and, if they wanted, would start avidly reading *Playboy*.

The adjutant's eyes shot up in surprise when I gave him the news. "Discharge? Oh." His voice trailed away, speechless, as I saluted, eyeing the black attaché case lying next to his desk as I walked out. When the SIB had searched all of my possessions, they'd found the attaché case. It was locked and for a very good reason. Inside was some very incriminating evidence, something that I didn't want anyone to see. Why they didn't just smash open the lock, I've never been able to understand. When I was questioned about the contents, I said that I'd left the key at my aunt's down in Worthing and it was only full of music. They accepted my explanation and told me that they would hand it over to the adjutant when I produced the keys; I could have it back once he'd looked inside. In fact, if they had looked inside, they'd have found some evidence, which may have made a big difference to their case against me. Inside, hidden in a brown envelope, were some homoerotic magazines. By today's standards the magazines were pretty mild, but at that time, quite explosive, and they could have been very dangerous for me had they been seen.

Life went on, each day seeming to last longer and longer as I waited. One day, something happened that would stay with me for the rest of my life. I was standing outside of the barrack block as a squad of men approached. I didn't realise until too late that it was my boys on the way to the education centre. I had no choice but to stand my ground as they approached. The junior NCO in charge of the squad saw me. He was a bright, friendly lad called Roland and as they marched past he gave the order, 'Eyes left!' as if I were an officer. To a man, the squad turned their heads towards me. It was Roland's way of saying, "We're sorry for what's happened to you, Corp, but we're on your side." I smiled and nodded as they marched past, my spirits momentarily lifted.

Before I left the army I learned that the boys had given the young recruit who I'd chatted up a rough time for grassing on me. I was sorry for that – I'd used him, and he was merely a means to an end. That sounds terribly cold, calculating and even callous. My decision to act in the way that I did that night, however, was a sub-conscious one, brought on by my guilt over Alex, something that I didn't realise until many years afterwards.

The uncertainty of it all took its toll and relentlessly ground me down. The psychological torture became unbearable as I waited to discover my fate, never sure what was about to happen next.

One of the most humiliating experiences that I've ever been through happened at this time. There was to be a Corporals' mess dinner and I had no choice but to attend. As I walked into that mess hall, everyone knew about me, and even my fellow band instructors ignored me as I sat down at the table and looked fixedly at my plate. It was an absolute nightmare. I picked at my food, being totally ostracised by my fellow corporals, and not one person showed me any kindness that night. The final humiliation came after the dinner. During my service I'd played at numerous officers' and sergeants' mess dinners. They would never have considered having a stripper as entertainment. Why, then, did someone decide that it would be appropriate for the corporals to have one performing that night? I have nothing at all against strippers, but a mess dinner isn't, in my opinion, a suitable venue, and it devalued the dignity of the occasion. But a stripper they had, and I became the focus of her attention. I think that I was set up. If not, why should I, out of a room full of men, become the one person that she made a bee line for? I hope that those men are proud of themselves and that they obtained plenty of satisfaction at my distress and unease. She came directly towards me and shoved her huge bosoms directly into my face. All that I could do was to sit there and take it, as those morons looked on in delight. After that I left as soon as I could. They

149

didn't know it, but they'd done me a favour. As I walked into my room, I slammed the door behind me, full of a blind and terrible rage. They'd forced me to make a decision and nothing would make me change my mind. There was just one thing that I had to do first.

My alarm went off at 5.00 am and the events of the previous night came flooding back with my anger in no way diminished, as I got up and dressed. The orderly room was the centre of the camp administration and home to the various administrators, including the adjutant. I quietly walked into the deserted and quiet entrance hall, and made my way down to the end of the corridor. The door to the adjutant's office stood open and my case lay just by the side of his desk. My heart was beating like a bass drum as I walked over, picked it up and unlocked it. I put my hand inside and took out the brown envelope containing the incriminating gay material. I quickly re-locked it and put it back by the side of the desk and walked out. As I approached the entrance, the envelope tucked underneath my arm, someone came through the door. I almost jumped out of my skin, as I was faced by a young lance corporal, who I knew well.

He looked at me sheepishly, and said quietly, "I'm glad that I've seen you, Dave." He hesitated, showing no surprise that I should be there so early in the morning and with no interest in the envelope. "About last night. I'm sorry." "I bet you fucking well are, you're all a load of moronic bastards," I said, my face flushed with anger. "Jesus Christ almighty," I continued, "do you people have no humanity? I hope that you all got a lot of satisfaction out of it." Before I could continue, he placed his hand on my arm, and said almost inaudibly, "No, Dave, I mean it. I'm sorry. You see you and I both play for the same team. If ever you want..." his voice trailed away.

My voice filled with anger and wanting to wound I snarled, "So you're a fucking queer too, are you? Just like me. Thanks for your kind invitation, but at this moment I'd rather screw a sheep, now get the fuck out of my way." I pushed past him and walked away. The truth was that, given another set of circumstances, I would have loved to have taken him up on the offer. The poor lad was just in the wrong place at the wrong time that morning.

That lunchtime I went into Royston and got rid of the evidence. Now I was ready to do what I'd been planning since the previous evening. I wanted an end to this, one way or another, and was determined to get it. That afternoon, I sat in my office and waited. I heard the major approach and as he walked into his office, I stood and walked towards his door, the humiliation of last night still burning brightly in my brain.

"Come in," he called as I knocked and entered. "Ah, Corporal Spencer. What can I do for you?" "Sir," I replied calmly, "I have to admit that I'm at the end of my tether. I've been humiliated enough and can't take anymore. If I may ask, sir," I said quietly, "how would you feel in my place? Having to walk around day in and day out, made to feel like something less than human. All that I want, sir, is a decision. Are they going to lock me up and throw away the key, or are they going to let me go? That's all that I want to know, sir." I stood silently, as this humane and decent man looked at me. He nodded his head up and down slowly and thoughtfully as he said, "You're quite right, Corporal Spencer. They're acting like barbarians, or worse. Leave it with me." "Thank you, sir," I said and walked quietly out of the door with a feeling of relief. As I sat down, I heard the telephone being lifted and a number being dialled. I waited.

"Hello Captain... It's Major... here. Tell me, just what the bloody hell is going on with Corporal Spencer's case. I don't give a damn. This has dragged on for long enough. Someone down there is acting no better than a Nazi. Listen, we both know that the SIB has no case against him. If they had, he'd have been charged weeks ago. Now get off your backside,

Captain, and do something about it." The sound of the receiver hitting the telephone echoed around the office.

Three days later, my discharge papers came through.

I marched into the adjutant's office, halted and saluted. "I've come for my case, sir," I said.

He looked at me, "We never did see inside there, did we Corporal Spencer?"

"No, sir. I have the keys now. Would you like to have a look?" I asked, innocently.

"That won't be necessary," he said, as I picked it up and left the room, knowing that it would be pointless to offer him my hand.

I was never charged with any crime. Just how thorough the SIB investigation against me had been, I'll never know. I do know that they went to the school of music and interviewed Ian. He told them nothing. One thing is sure. They couldn't have found any serious evidence against me, for if they had, the ending of this story would be very different. In the eyes of the army and military law, I was a homosexual, and that was crime enough. In hindsight, it's possible that Colonel 'L's' report on me had put doubt into their minds on the whole subject of my sexuality, and as they had no more than the recruit's evidence to go on, decided to drop the matter. If so, the man did me a big favour. I had the advantage, because no serving soldier would ever admit to having had a sexual relationship with me, for they too, would have been charged. My discharge papers were marked, "Services no longer required."

I was free. The gates of the prison that I'd created in my mind over the past twelve years swung open, and now I had to make a choice. It was quite simple. Do I face up to my sexuality and get on with living my life as a gay man, or do I stay in denial? The choice was mine and mine alone.

Dawn

The early morning sun streamed in through the patterned curtains as they gently billowed, pushed by the light breeze. My eyes slowly opened as I drowsily realised that today was Sunday and a lie-in was perfectly in order. I looked around the drab little room, my arm snaking over towards the bedside table and my cigarettes. Lighting up, I inhaled deeply and reflected lazily on the events of the last year. My gaze focused on the cheap print hanging on the opposite wall. My new home was a bed-sit in the Erdington district of Birmingham, and like my little house-in-the-sky in Richmond, I loved it. My fears had begun to subside and had finally disappeared in the months after my discharge. At last I was beginning to feel at peace with myself. The guilt that I felt was still there deep within, but somehow was subdued and bearable. Anyone thinking that I'd spent the past few months in a sexual orgy, rampaging like a horny bull all over the Birmingham gay scene, would be wrong. I wasn't ready for that. Instead my time had been spent in quiet reflection and contemplation on what direction my life was going to take. In my heart I knew that I could go only one way, and I was slowly heading in the right direction. It only needed a little push and I would be there.

For a short while after leaving the army, I settled in Redditch with my parents, but quickly realised that having my own space was essential and started to look around for somewhere to live. Firstly, though, I needed a job and was totally unsuited to anything on offer in 'Civvie Street'. If I'd left the army in the normal way, I'd have been entitled to a resettlement course and learned to be a painter and decorator or some such thing. There wasn't much use for an ex-army clarinet player and I had no illusions about playing with the Birmingham Symphony Orchestra. "Welcome to the real world," I reflected, as I studied the situations vacant column in the *Birmingham Mail*. At this point, fate was to take a hand, and not for the last time. I applied for a job with a well-known security firm who paid peanuts. I took up my duties sitting behind a reception desk in the *Prudential* building in central Birmingham. It was mind-numbingly boring, as an endless parade of people traipsed past, stopping to ask me the way to the household insurance department. I got to know the people who worked there well, and at least had the consolation of being able to cruise the office lads as they went about their business.

Each morning and afternoon a smartly dressed man (usually a different person each day) would come in and head for the 'Customs and Excise' offices on the second floor. They wore grey suits with a maroon tie, on which the gold symbol of the *Bank of England* was printed. These men were all members of the *Bank of England* security team and were mostly ex-servicemen. The bank had their own security force and wouldn't employ an outside firm. A job with the country's leading bank was to be prized and was much sought after. I was amazed to discover that one of these men had been a corporal in my own regiment. No wonder he seemed familiar. One morning, one of these security men came in and stopped by my desk. "Morning, Dave," he said, offering me a cigarette from an open packet. Before I could reply, he continued, "Do you know, there's a place going over at the bank?"

My ears went up and I looked at him with interest. Jim had been in the Royal Navy, and I'm convinced that he and I were in someway linked, as he was to play a big part in another life-changing event in my life. "You're kidding," I said.
"I'm not, mate. Give them a ring now. Go on, here's the number."

I hesitated, and if he hadn't have stood watching me, I doubt very much if I would have bothered. Thankfully he was insistent as I reluctantly lifted the phone and dialled the proffered number. I explained who I was and that I'd just left the army, obviously not giving any reasons, and asked if I could apply for the vacant post. Whenever a serviceman leaves the armed forces, he receives a small, red book. Inside is written the serviceman's complete military history, which includes a reference. The references of military conduct range from 'exemplary' to 'unsatisfactory'. Mine was exemplary and the reference, written by my old friend the major, couldn't have been better if I'd have written it myself. It was superb. However, when you turn the page you see reasons for discharge: 'Services No Longer Required." But what could I do? Short of tearing the offending page out, which would have been illegal, there wasn't much to be done, and I duly handed it in at the front door and waited. This time, however, I was determined to be ready for them. One morning I received a letter on embossed, *Bank of England* notepaper, telling me to report for an interview. I was ushered into a plush office on the ground floor. Sitting behind a large desk were two smartly-dressed men who eyed me up and down as I sat facing them. After a few pleasantries we got down to business and I immediately went on the attack – metaphorically speaking, that is. "I suppose that you've noticed the reason for discharge, sir?" I asked.

The one man looked at the other, and replied, "Yes we had. The reference is very good, but..."
His voice trailed off, as he looked at me expectantly. "Yes, sir, if I could explain?" It was at this point that I started to mix fact with fiction. I told them that I'd had an operation for a hernia, brought about by my playing whilst marching up-hill – fact. I continued by saying that the army had offered me a discharge, but could only do so on the grounds of services no longer required – bullshit! They seemed to accept that and the rest of the interview went smoothly. I left the bank that day and prayed. The next few weeks were torture as I anxiously waited

for the morning post to arrive. Then one morning I received a letter telling me to report to a doctor in Edgbaston for a medical. I phoned my dad and told him. He wisely said, "Son, you've got the job." And so I had.

My heart was singing the day that I walked into the bank and reported for duty. I'd arrived and landed myself a very prestigious job. *The Bank of England*, even in the mid-seventies, seemed to be in a time warp, and was both Victorian and Conservative with a capital 'C'. If at the interview those two men had suspected that I was homosexual and had known the true reasons for my leaving the army, I never would have got the job.

For reasons of security I will not divulge any details of the job itself, but my time at the bank was very happy. We worked a shift system, of course, as the bank was guarded 24 hours a day for 365 days a year. We would do three nights, followed by four free days, which was great for your social life, and we were well paid. There were enormous perks to the job, like very favourable mortgages. All in all it was a job to be envied.

As I lay in bed that sunny Sunday morning in 1976, I reflected that my life was starting to get better and I was reasonably happy. There were still things that I had to sort out within myself, but I felt that at last I was starting to make some progress. I got up, put on the kettle and turned on the radio. By doing a simple thing like turning on the radio, little was I to know that my life was about to turn direction again. I would at last find a way that would ultimately lead to peace, contentment and love.

The sounds of a discordant contemporary piece of music filled the air, setting my teeth on edge. This didn't suit my mood at all and I hastily lent over and re-tuned the radio station. As my usual choice of music was classical, the radio was set permanently on Radio 3, but the finger of fate made me turn to a pop music station. If when I'd first turned the radio on, there'd been a piece of Beethoven playing, I'd have left it tuned to that station and would never have heard the interview that followed. I sat on the settee with half an ear listening to the music while I sipped at a cup of tea and tried to decide what to do with the rest of the day. A visit to the pub would be a good idea, I thought to myself, followed by a Chinese take-away from across the road. The station was *BRMB*, the local Birmingham radio, and the DJ's announcement, when it came, made me jump forward, depositing a copious amount of tea onto the already stained carpet. "Next up, ladies and gentlemen, we have a nice fellow from Birmingham gay switchboard to talk to us. Stand by, Sam will be talking to us, after this..." The strains of Abba's 'Dancing Queen' filled the air, as I listened impatiently, wondering if the DJ's choice of record was deliberate.

The interview that followed kept me riveted to my seat. Sam talked about the work of the switchboard and the urgent need for volunteers. "Volunteers be damned," I thought, selfishly, as I waited with impatience to be told the telephone number, something I knew that would surely follow. I wasn't disappointed, as I hastily scribbled it down and turned off the radio, staring into space thoughtfully. The rest of the day was spent in turmoil, as I made up my mind, that no matter what, I was going to make that phone call. The call box was in the street just outside my front door, as I paced up and down, waiting for the old biddy already inside to hurry up and finish. After what seemed an age she walked out and I quickly strode in, my heart thumping inside my chest. I dialled and waited. The receiver was lifted almost immediately, and a voice said, "Hello, Birmingham gay switchboard... speaking. How may I help you?"

Taking a deep breath, I started to speak. How long I was on that phone for I have no real idea; I do know that I fed the coin box on at least three occasions, hardly pausing for breath. At the end, a note of pleading in my voice, I said, "Look, I'd really like to speak to someone face to face about this. Will you help?"

There was a silence for a moment, before the person at the other end replied, "Can you call back in about an hour's time, Dave?"

I said that I would and hung up, my heart racing. Walking back up to my bed-sit, I closed the door and poured myself a stiff whisky, my hands trembling slightly as the fiery liquid hit the back of my throat. Eventually I calmed down slightly and waited, the minutes ticking slowly by as I nervously glanced at my watch.

When I rang back, the voice at the other end of the line said, in a light and extremely friendly tone, "Hi, Dave. It's all arranged and they're very much looking forward to meeting you. Can you go to this address tomorrow at two o'clock?" He gave me the address of a house in Moseley, as I hastily scribbled it down. "The person to ask for is either Joe or Sam, and good luck." I thanked him profusely and hung up, and as I slowly walked up the street to the nearest pub a feeling of immense relief passed over me. That night I drank slowly, feeling happier than I had in a very long time.

I took the bus the next day and found the correct road, a row of Victorian terraced houses beginning to run to seed, the paint starting to peel. Many of the houses in the row had been turned into flats and bed-sits, home to a countless number of students. I rang the bell and waited, feeling strangely calm and at peace, as if I knew that something momentous was about to happen. A tall, slim man with a trimmed beard, wearing jeans, opened the door and smiled. His eyes sparkled and he gave an air of quiet confidence, reminding me of every one's idea of one of Christ's disciples. Holding out his hand, he said in a soft and gentle voice, "Hello, you must be Dave. I'm Joe, and you're very welcome."

I took the proffered hand and smiled, feeling instantly at ease in his presence as he led me up the stairs. As we entered a large living room, another man, this one a little younger, stood and introduced himself as Sam. Joe apologised that there were two of them present, but as they didn't know me they thought that it would be safer, joking that I could be a mad axe-murderer. I owe those two men a great debt. I sat for hours, drinking coffee and pouring out my heart to them, telling them everything and omitting nothing. They sat and listened, their eyes watching me closely, hanging on to every word that I uttered. It occurred to me that both Joe and Sam were the first openly gay men that I'd ever met. They seemed totally at ease with themselves, and I learned that Joe was a preacher in the Metropolitan Community Church, which explained his air of tranquillity. Over the next few years, Joe was to become a friend and teacher to me. I remember with gratitude his arms encircling me one night, giving me comfort, as if I was a child, and expecting nothing in return.

Finally, exhausted, I sat back and looked from one to the other, a feeling of total relief overwhelming me. For the first time ever, I'd been able to talk about my inner fears and myself to people who really understood my problems. They were homosexuals, just like me, and both had experienced people's distaste and hate during the course of their lives.

Joe turned to me, and said with quiet compassion, "You poor chap. You've had a really rough ride, haven't you? Well, now it's over. I promise you one thing – from now on you'll never be isolated or alone again."

I just sat there facing them, with tears streaming down my face, unable to say anything.

To say that my life changed that day would be an understatement. I discovered a world that I could only have dreamed of, and I revelled in it. *The Jester*, a gay pub in the centre of Birmingham, became my second home, and it's still there to this day, as if indestructible. I'd sit at the bar, my foot tapping to the beat of 'Dancing Queen', a tune that I grew to love. Joe and Sam were true to their word and introduced me to many people. You cannot begin to understand what it was like for me, to be surrounded by other men who were the same and who didn't give a damn who knew it. The closet door had finally been thrown open in 1967, and God help anyone who tried to close it again. The queers were out and spoiling for a fight.

My first meeting with the more militant gays came as a shock to me. They were mostly students and members of 'The Gay Liberation Front'. Like students throughout history, they grabbed their cause with a verve that was frightening to behold. They wore tight, flared jeans, tee shirts emblazoned with slogans like, 'Glad To Be Gay', their hair flowing down their backs in waves. To someone like me, someone so used to the rigid discipline of military society, they were more than a little frightening. Neil was one of them, an incredibly tall and handsome young student from Bristol. He was my first legal lover, but we had little in common and soon drifted apart. His left wing politics irked me, while at the same time my drinking irked him. I didn't give a damn. I was enjoying myself – to hell with everyone else.

One evening I was talking to Joe with the jukebox throbbing in the background, making it almost impossible to be heard. "Joe," I shouted, "I want to give something back." I was a bit pissed and feeling happy with myself.
"What do you mean, give something back," he shouted, his eyes twinkling.
"Just that. I want to do something useful. Listen, Joe. I'm too old to be a student, and militancy doesn't come easily to me. It's all of that military training."
"Good Lord, Dave. How old are you, all of 27?"
"I know how old I am, but I want to do something. I can't sit here doing nothing until I'm an old queen," I said, with all of the seriousness of a man with six pints under his belt.

"You already are an old queen. Anyway, what do you have in mind?"

"I want to join gay switchboard," I announced, solemnly.

"You're on. I'll train you. And Dave, I think that you'll be very good at it."

He was as good as his word. He'd been on London switchboard for years and knew what he was doing. We spent hours together going through every imaginable scenario at his flat in Moseley, until one day he announced that he thought I was ready and could be let loose under his supervision. The switchboard in those days was situated in the gay centre, an old building in Digbeth. The centre was quite innovative and ahead of its time, a place where gay men and women could meet, drink coffee and pass a few hours in the evenings. The room housing the switchboard, a misnomer really as there was only one phone line, was up on the first floor and strictly off limits to everybody except the operators. I sat there on my first evening, scared. I realised that I had a great responsibility, as not everyone out there was 'glad to be gay'. I very quickly learned that what I said could make a great difference to people who were as screwed up as I'd been just a few months previously.

We had our fair share of hoax and abusive calls, or the odd visiting gay person who wanted to know where the best bars were. Most of the calls that I took, however, were from men who were having great difficulty with their sexual identity. How I empathised with them, and if I could help, then I would. I can honestly say that I did what I could, and chose my words with care, quickly learning that it was often better to listen while they poured their hearts out than to say anything. God, I got so angry. These were human beings who felt worthless and were despised by an uncaring society, many of whom would have liked nothing better to put us all back into the closet and throw away the key – or worse!

Sadly, in that respect, little has changed over the past thirty years. From the so-called educated men who spill their bile over into column inches in national newspapers, claiming to speak for Middle-England (if they do truly speak for Middle-England, then I thank God that I no longer live there), and people who profess to be Christians yet despise us (while piously getting down on their knees to worship every Sunday – so much for their Christian love – that is one of the reasons that I haven't set foot in a church to attend a service for years, despite having deeply-held religious beliefs), to the tattooed young thugs who stalk the towns and cities of Britain (and who would look very much at home wearing the brown shirts, jackboots and swastika armbands of their Nazi heroes). Emotive language I know, and it would be unfair to generalise, but there are still far too many people with the mind-set of those described above. First and foremost, we are human beings and have the same rights to our dignity and humanity as any other member of society.

In Germany 70 years ago this year, the Nazis came to power and it was they who decided who was not acceptable in their society. It was the Nazis who coined the word *'Untermensch'*, and weeded out all of those they deemed inferior and unfit to live. The final result of such thinking was Auschwitz.

One evening I was sitting in the switchboard room when the phone rang. I lifted the receiver, gave the usual response and waited. I spoke to a young man who said that he desperately needed our help. After I'd listened to him for a while, I asked him if he would be prepared to meet me for a chat. He readily agreed, on the condition that we didn't meet anywhere that was remotely gay. The next evening, we met in an ordinary pub in the centre of Birmingham. I was surprised at how young he was, in his very early twenties. He was married and already had two small children. As we drank our pints, he explained his problem. A salesman, he was on the road everyday and his own boss. "The trouble is, I'm gay," he explained, "and knew that I was on the day that I walked down the aisle. I'm living a lie and it's killing me." He continued, "I've started using public toilets to meet other men for sex. It's anonymous, you see."

I nodded, knowing full well what it's like to live a lie. "You know," I said, "you're playing a dangerous game. The police are well aware of these places and keep them under surveillance. It's only a matter of time before you fall into the net. If you're arrested, they'll make damn sure that the local press are inside the court when your case comes up, and then your name will be plastered all over the newspaper."

"I know, but what can I do?"

"You could always come clean, admit that you've made a big mistake and separate."

"Oh, yeh, and what am I going to tell everyone – that I'm a queer."

"But you are," I replied, "and if you're arrested, they'll find out anyway. Listen, you'd be better off if you went to a gay bar. At least that way you're not likely to be picked up by the police. I've heard of men in your position having discreet relationships like that." I admit that I was out of my depth and didn't really know what I could do to help him. He sighed and muttered, "What a fucking mess."

I couldn't help but agree, as I silently studied him. He was a good-looking blond lad, who'd got himself into a mess and didn't know how to get out of it. He had a wife and two small children, and it was all going to end in tears. The only thing that I could suggest was that he meet one of our team. The chap I had in mind was a married man with a family, whose wife knew all about the situation and accepted it, something that I could never understand. He would often bring his daughter to the gay centre. I suggested that they meet, as my colleague had more experience in that area, and the lad agreed. To be honest, I was relieved. As we left the pub that night, I turned to him and said, "If you don't mind my asking – you say that you knew you were gay on the day you walked down the aisle?"

"That's right."

"So why did you marry?"

He looked me straight in the eye and replied, "Because that's what was expected of me. Anyway, I didn't want to be branded a queer."

I never set eyes on him again.

Sunlight

I fell in love. It happened in an instant; one second sitting there, the next, total, irrevocable, love. I was in the *Jester* one cold early December night in 1976. I can tell you the exact date, the 10ᵗʰ. It was relatively quiet that evening, as I sat toying with a glass of lager, my mind elsewhere. I glanced up as three pairs of legs descended the stairs and the rest of the bodies came into view. The last of the three young men who entered was tall and slim with light brown wavy hair, and it was he who immediately became the focus of my attention. Never before in my life, and never since, have I experienced a feeling like it. I had an overwhelming need to talk to him. This wasn't anything sexual, and the thought of sex with this attractive young man seemed an insult to him, as if I wasn't worthy to even have such ideas. What would this young god want to do with a fat, unattractive queer like me, I asked myself. The other two people I knew well. Stephen looked after the finances of the Gay Centre and I'd often spoken to him. I knew his partner, John, too, but the whole focus of my very being was concentrated on their companion, and I had to talk to him, no matter what. He seemed a little ill at ease, as if not used to grotty little pubs like this, being there only under sufferance. They ordered their drinks and sat down in a quiet corner. Slowly I left the bar and walked over towards them, my heart beating. As I approached, Stephen and John looked up and smiled. "Hello," I said, "Do you mind if I join you?" "Of course not, Dave," said Stephen, "This is Martin."

I smiled and held out my hand as I said, "Hello Martin." Feeling like a tongue-tied young girl on her first date, I so wanted to make a good impression, but ended up tying myself in knots and feeling stupid and inarticulate. I know that we talked about the ballet and I could feel Martin's eyes on me, watching me closely. He didn't say much, but I discovered that he was an English teacher, which made me feel even more inferior, as I asked myself what anyone like him would want to do with an uneducated idiot like me. I was totally besotted and, had he asked me, would gladly have thrown myself in the canal. As the evening went on, I tried to find the courage to ask him out, but feared being rejected. As they stood and prepared to leave, my heart beating like a steam-hammer in my chest, I tentatively said, "Martin, would you like to meet me for dinner one evening?"

I waited for his response, feeling awkward and ill at ease, as he replied, "Thanks, Dave, I'd like that, when?" I couldn't believe it. He'd said yes and my heart lifted, as I said, "How about Friday. I'll meet you here at 7.30. We can go to *Cassidy's*." "Yes, I'd like that," he said smiling, "I'll see you then. Goodbye." The others nodded and walked towards the stairs, and as I watched them leave my heart sang.

The next few days dragged. God how they dragged, as I waited impatiently for Friday night and our first date. I arrived early, nervously sipping a drink, my heart filled with fear in case he'd had second thoughts. I needn't have worried, as he appeared smack on time. When I asked him if he'd like a drink, he refused, as if in a hurry to leave. Over the course of the evening, I discovered that Mart had never before been inside a gay bar, and had only gone to please Stephen, his oldest friend. He admitted to me that he'd had no intention of ever going there again. Over the years I've often thanked God for allowing me to be inside the *Jester* that night, for if I hadn't, we'd never have met. We started to relax in each other's company as the evening progressed, discovering a mutual love of music. We walked slowly home on that cold

December night, stopping at the off-licence to by a bottle of sherry. I laugh now, as I'd have much preferred a six-pack of lager, but didn't dare say so.

Number 10, Ampton Road was a place that I grew to love as much as Martin did over the years, a beautiful old Victorian house, set in its own grounds. I was over-awed at the grandeur of the place, as he led me through the front door and up the stairs to his flat on the first floor. The lounge seemed enormous, with its high ceiling and tasteful furnishings. We sat and talked for what seemed like hours. I realised that I was very much in love with this handsome young man, who, at 23, was four years my junior. He sat at my feet, his resting head on my lap as I stroked his hair, realising that he was as much in love with me, as I was with him.

That night we made love; for Martin, the first time. I say love, because that's exactly what it was, an act of love. Anything that had happened to me before was meaningless, as if it had never happened, and my life changed forever that night. The slate was wiped clean, and the self-hate that had haunted me for so many years disappeared for good, never to reappear.

Stephen was absolutely horrified. "Have you gone mad?" he asked Martin, when he announced that I was to move in. "You've only known Dave for five minutes and you're planning on living together." Martin was adamant and wouldn't be moved. He was as sure as I was that we'd made the right decision. I moved in just before Christmas. It's ironic that the very people who thought Martin unwise have long since split with their various partners and gone their separate ways. This year the two of us will celebrate 28 years together.

The Christmas that followed was the happiest that I've ever had and seemed unending. First I had to meet the new 'in-laws'. I put on my regimental blazer and tie and waited with a great deal of apprehension for them to arrive. His father, Steve, and I took to each other immediately, as we both shared a military background and had a lot in common. Over the years Steve Jackson has raised over £30,000 for the British Legion, and I would often see him standing outside *Rackhams* with his collecting box, wearing his father's medals with pride. Steve's father, before his death on the battlefield in France, had been awarded both the DCM and MM for gallantry. He was killed in action in October 1917.

Beattie Jackson, on the other hand, eyed me with some suspicion, and who can blame her? Like all mothers, she guarded her youngest son and was determined to look after his best interests. Now, bless her, an old lady in her 90s, I like to think that she holds me in some affection.

Mart, Steven and John went off on their annual pilgrimage to the carol concert in Liverpool Cathedral the weekend before Christmas, while I went and did some shopping and stocked up with booze for the festive season. People seemed to be popping in to visit all over the holiday, and I remember how happy we both were. One evening the Spencer family descended *en-masse* and straight away took Martin to their hearts. I was touched when my mother turned to me and said, "I have a new son." Since that day, he's been treated as a much-loved member of the family.

Number 10 – what a household; Jock and Nella Wilson, a nice old couple who looked on themselves as being the guardians of the house, occupied the whole of the ground floor. Next door to us, on the first floor, lived a delightfully eccentric old lady called Katie Kettle, a retired music teacher who claimed to have written the national anthem of some obscure country that no one had ever heard of. She was a short, fat woman, with a cherubic face and masses of white, curly hair – imagine Margaret Rutherford as Miss Marple. Katie had this enormously fat, black cat, and she was for ever laboriously making her way slowly down the stairs, walking stick in hand, in search of the wretched feline. 'Lucy', the above mentioned cat, was so fat that Katie would lower it to the ground from the first floor in a basket tied to a piece of rope. One morning, the old dear found it lying on its back in the garden, with its legs in the air, unable to turn over because of its enormous size.

On the top floor we had the newly-weds, Karen and Ashley, a lovely young couple in their early twenties. Both Mart and I lusted over Ashley and would spy on him through the bedroom window as he washed his car. Just across the courtyard, Mrs Proctor was in residence. She'd been a matron at one of the Birmingham hospitals – the old-fashioned type, who have long since disappeared from the NHS. And there was of course us, the two young gays. They should have made a TV sit-com based on the occupants of that house – it would have been a smash hit.

We had some wonderful parties at number 10 in those days, and all of the various people in the house would be invited. Jock and Nella would never come to the actual party, but would come up for half an hour beforehand. They would arrive immaculately dressed, as if going to a Buckingham Palace garden party, have a glass of sherry and leave. Nella once remarked to Martin that she thought it very nice to see so many young men, as girls could cause so much trouble. Katie wouldn't have missed one of our parties for the world. She always wore a long flowing evening gown that had seen better days, an effect that was somewhat spoiled when you looked down at her feet and noticed her zip-up ('bootie') type house slippers. She would be ensconced regally in an upright chair in the corner of the large room, holding a glass of sherry and lasciviously eyeing the gorgeous young men who were always present. I like to think of dear Katie, sitting up in heaven, glass of sherry in hand, ogling the angels – may God bless her.

At one party we invited some of the student types from the Gay Liberation Front. They stood in a group in one corner, their faces wreathed with jealousy at our perceived wealth. The next morning we discovered evidence of their venom and dislike. A nice table in the corner of the room had been used as an ashtray. They were never invited again.

169

Two things happened on a Saturday night: *Dallas* and the *Grosvenor*, in that order. *Dallas* was a popular American TV series, and we were hooked and never missed an episode. *The Grosvenor* was a large gay complex with hotel facilities. I look on the hours that we spent there as some of the happiest of my life. There was a large bar with a baby grand piano and a pianist to go with it. The old queens, me included, would stand around it late at night, singing Gilbert and Sullivan and songs from the shows. Next door, there was a disco and we spent hours dancing, usually ending up soaked in sweat. We often met our two oldest gay friends, Barry and Brian, who both deserve a mention here. One Saturday evening the two of us were sitting in the bar having a drink. Martin happened to glance up and froze. He nudged me, and said with some alarm, "Oh, Christ, look over there."

"What is it?" I said.

"Those two lads. They're sixth formers from the school."

"Do you want to leave?" I asked.

"It's too late now, they've already seen me. Shit!"

David and Martin

It must be understood that Mart was a schoolteacher, and although things had changed somewhat, 'homosexual' equalled paedophile to many people (and sadly still does to this day). It was with some trepidation that he went into school the following Monday morning, but he needn't have worried. The two lads made an unspoken deal with Mart, which said, "We won't tell anyone that you're gay, as long as you say nothing about us being in there in the first place." Both parties kept their side of the bargain.

I look back on those days as a huge voyage of discovery and adventure, an adventure that Mart and I shared together. Only two years previously I'd been inside a prison of my own making, and now my life had changed out of all recognition. In many ways both Martin and I shared mutual experiences, the gay scene being as foreign to him as it was to me. During those years I took him on his first ever trip abroad and showed him the continental way of life, so different from our own, and one that in many ways I envied. We started a long love affair with that Mecca of all things gay, Amsterdam, a love affair that has long since passed away. In short, we took a journey of self-discovery, hand-in-hand together, and learned much about each other.

I was to have one last contact with the army at around this time. I started to work for the gay counselling group, 'Friend'. After a period of training I would meet gay men who had problems of one kind or another; we would talk and I would try to help. The bond that could grow between a man and a councillor was quite amazing. One of my clients, if I can use that word in such a context, was a man of extraordinary intelligence and I quickly realised that he needed an expertise far greater than mine. Over a period of time, as he grew to trust me, I asked if he would consider seeing a psychiatrist. To my great surprise, he agreed, on the condition that I went with him. Friend had a doctor working with them, a man that I both knew and admired. I spoke to him and we arranged an appointment away from any hospital, so as to reassure my client. He was quickly diagnosed with manic-depression and a course of treatment was suggested. There is no cure for the illness, but it can be controlled by the use of drugs, such as Lithium. Sadly my client refused any treatment and continued to suffer huge mood swings as a result. He latched on to me and wouldn't let go. In many ways, Mart and I dreaded meeting him. He'd discovered that we did our shopping on Saturday mornings at *Tesco's* and always went for a drink at the pub afterwards. When he walked in, we would never know whether he was on a high or low that particular day. When he was on a high, he was indeed manic and over the top; on a low, he was depressive. Sadly, there was little to be done to help that man.

One evening Mart and I were sitting at home watching the television when the telephone rang. It was my boss from Friend. "Dave, we need your help," he said, "We've been contacted by a young soldier and you seem to be the ideal person to take on the case."

I immediately agreed, and it was arranged for the young man to come around to Ampton Road the next day. A taxi pulled up and out climbed a young, blond-haired lad of about 20. I let him in and we shook hands as I led him up the stairs and into the flat. He was a typical young squaddie, brash, with lots of rough charm. He was the kind of lad that you can see in any pub on a Saturday night. The first thing he said to me as we sipped our beer was that he'd told his dad that he was gay and had promptly been thrown out of the house for his trouble. He was determined that he was going to come out as homosexual to the army, no matter what the consequences. I advised caution, my mind on my own experiences, but he was adamant and wouldn't be moved. I admired him and racked my brains for the best way to help. As I sat there and looked back on my own experiences one man came to mind, the padre. During my own dark period, I'd found the padre to be sympathetic to my plight, and had often spoken to him. I realised that if he was determined to go through with it, the lad

172

should speak to the person most likely to listen to him with some sympathy. It was the best that I could come up with. We agreed that he should wait for a few days and that in the meantime I would write to the padre, using Friend headed notepaper. I did that, held my breath and waited a few days, giving the letter plenty of time to arrive. I phoned the padre one afternoon and explained who I was. He wasn't particularly communicative or friendly, not that I cared a damn, but told me that the matter was being taken care of. I thanked him and hung up.

Some time later I met the lad and asked him how he'd got on. He was full of beans and said that, thanks to me, he'd seen the padre and things had gone smoothly. Even the RSM was sympathetic, he explained, and a discharge was being arranged. "It'll be a 'services no longer required job'," he said, as I smiled and replied, "Welcome to the club."

There was still one more thing that I needed to do, and it was very important to me. I was going to come out as gay at the bank. I was sick of all of the pretence and lies. This was to be the final step. We used a rest room to have coffee in the morning before starting work, and I used this time to drop my bombshell. We were all sitting around the table, when I asked everyone for their attention. They looked at me curiously as I said, very quietly, with my heart beating, "I've got something that I want to tell you all." Now that I had their attention, I plunged on. "I want you all to know that I'm gay and that I'm living with my partner, Martin. I hope that this won't be a problem for anyone, but if it is, I'll understand."

I sat back and waited, my heart full of apprehension, but feeling strangely calm. There was a stunned silence, as everyone looked at me, until Mike, a good friend and highly respected by everyone, said, "Thanks for telling us Dave. We thought that you might be, but for myself, it makes no difference at all. You're still the good mate that you were five minutes ago." He looked around the table, as if challenging

173

anyone to disagree with him. My heart was filled with gratitude and we're still good friends to this day.

I had one violent reaction from our immediate boss, who'd served with the guards in London during his National Service and may have had stories of his own to tell. We had a head to head, but it soon blew over once he'd got used to the idea, and we were soon back together drinking in the pub at lunchtime. One man I admired above all others was a chap called Kevin. An Irish Catholic, he took me to one side, and very quietly and calmly told me that he could never agree with my lifestyle, but it was my life, and I should live it as I wished. That man was never once in any way nasty towards me and we worked together well.

Within minutes of outing myself, the bank was buzzing with the news, but I tried to carry on with my work as if nothing had happened, wondering what was going to happen next. I didn't have long to wait. It was suddenly announced that the head of bank security was going to make a visit the next day. In those days the bank always employed an ex high-ranking police officer as their head of security. This man was quite famous as the man who'd led the inquiry into what became known as the Cannock Chase murders. We were summoned one by one into his presence. Of course he was only there to see one person, me. However, he was obliged to go through the motions and I was duly called. I went in and sat down as he looked at me. He asked me how I liked working at the bank and how I was getting on. I told him that I was very happy and enjoyed my job. "I believe that you came out as gay yesterday," he said.
"That's right," I replied, "but that in no way affects the way that I do my job."
He nodded, and said, "Well, at least you can no longer be regarded as a security risk."
A flash of anger went through me like a bolt of lightning at that moment, as I leaned towards him, and said quietly, "I was never a security risk. Do you understand, never?"

He smiled, and said, "OK, Mr Spencer. Thank you for being so honest."
And that was the end of the matter.

Everyone soon accepted the new me and treated me no differently from anyone else. After that, we gave a number of dinner parties for the lads and their wives and generally had a good time. I was amused when one morning one of the cleaning ladies said, very quietly, "If you don't mind me asking – who out of the two of you, well you know, takes the lady's position?" I roared with laughter and politely told her to mind her own business.

At around this time, our eyes started to turn towards the European continent as a place to live. I can't give you a definitive reason for our wanting to do so – perhaps someone up there decided that it might be a good idea for us to go elsewhere, after all, neither of us had any experience of continental life, and my two years spent in Berlin hardly qualified me to be an expert. We even went so far as to contact a Belgian gay group and were invited to spend a weekend with them, the idea being that we'd have a look at the job situation while we were there. Of course, we had a whale of a time in the gay bars and clubs of Brussels, but never went anywhere near a job agency.

One morning around about the middle of 1979 I walked into work after a four-day rest period. I was drinking coffee when our old friend Jim, came into the room and joined me. "Eh, Dave," he said, "You know that you're always going on about living abroad?" I said yes, looking at him curiously. "A couple of days ago, in *The Daily Mail*, there was an ad for two messengers at the European Courts of Justice. I'm sure that the paper's still in the control room, why don't you go and have a look?" Jumping out of my chair, I headed towards the control room muttering, "Thanks, Jim." Sure enough it was there and I feverishly opened the paper looking for the ad. It read: "Two messengers required at the European Courts of

175

Justice. Fluent English and a satisfactory knowledge of a second European language required." I gazed at it thoughtfully and wondered if I stood any chance at all. If Jim hadn't mentioned that ad, I'd have remained in blissful ignorance and the chance would have been lost. Sadly, still a young man, Jim was to die in the mid-eighties – may he rest in peace.

That evening I showed Mart the ad and we had a serious conversation about the benefits of moving. He was unhappy as a teacher, and whilst I had a good job, the prospect of having to work nights and weekends for years to come didn't attract me that much. At that time those of us at the bank thought that the job would be for life. The Birmingham branch was closed down during the 1980s and everyone was made redundant. That evening Martin and I decided that we'd both apply for the post, and if one of us got it, then we'd both go. There was, however, a problem, the second language. Whilst Martin had an 'O'-Level in French, I only spoke 'double-Dutch' – not much good. We hatched a plan, and Martin agreed to give me some French lessons. He argued that the European Community was such a large bureaucracy that it would take months before either of us was called for an interview. For myself, I didn't think that Mart stood much chance, as he was far too highly educated, whereas I, on the other hand, might just be accepted. With my army and bank background, I thought that I stood a good chance. I promised myself this time that they'd only get to see the parts of my army references that I wanted them to see.

We duly sent off the forms and waited. Sure enough, Mart received a letter turning him down, whilst I heard nothing. Each afternoon, after work, I'd spend a couple of hours trying to master the basics of the French language.

Each day I'd say a little prayer as I walked to catch the bus to work. The time dragged on and I heard nothing, until one morning a buff envelope landed on the doormat. It told me to report to Kensington Palace Gardens for an interview. Martin reasoned, accurately as it turned out, that there were only so many questions that I was likely to be asked at an interview. We sat together and compiled a list of about twenty questions and worked on them. The interview was for 9.00 am and so we booked ourselves into a gay hotel in Earls Court. The next morning Martin and I walked over to Kensington Palace Gardens, and I remember being incredibly calm as we said goodbye and I headed, yet again, to my date with destiny. If I could have kissed Martin then, as we parted, I would have done.

I was the first to arrive and the first in. As I entered, there were three men sitting at a table facing me – the jury. I shook hands with them all and sat facing them. The man in charge was a Belgian who spoke fluent English. To his left sat an Englishman, whilst on the right sat a man that I was later to learn was a German. He looked at me, but said nothing. We talked for a while, the Englishman showing great interest in my army career. He told me that he'd served twenty-two years in the army and had finished his service as a WO1. I sighed with relief and thanked God that I'd only sent photocopies of my army references. If this man had seen the originals, he'd have guessed immediately that something was not quite right.

The moment that I'd been dreading arrived, when the German interviewer asked me in French, what my interests were. To my relief and great surprise, I realised that I not only understood him but was also able to reply. He stumped me on one question, when he asked me something about French cooking. When I was unable to reply, the Belgian said something to him in German and the interview was brought to a close. They thanked me and we all shook hands. As I walked out of that room, I knew that I'd got the job. To my amazement, I realised that the whole procedure had taken no more than half an hour and, in need of a drink, I headed towards the nearest pub. Unfortunately, I was too early and they were closed!

As I walked back into the hotel, the owner looked at me and said, "That was quick." I beamed, and replied, full of confidence, "I'll tell you what. Mart and I will stay here on our way to Luxembourg." "Wow, you're very confident," he said. I nodded, and replied, "I am."

The weeks dragged on and I heard nothing, but reasoned that no news was good news. One morning, during the school holidays, I was sitting in the control room gazing at the bank of televisions in front of me, when the telephone rang. Mike answered it and turning to me said, "It's Martin," as he handed me the receiver. I was surprised as Martin rarely contacted me at the bank. "Hello." I said, my heart pounding. Martin replied excitedly, "You've had a call from Luxembourg. Can you contact a Mr Barnett from the personnel department, here's the number." He gave me the number breathlessly as I quickly wrote it down, said, "Thank you," and hung up. Turning to Mike, I said, "I think I've got the job."

I went to see my boss and asked if I could phone Luxembourg. "No, son, you go home and do it. You should be with Mart. Don't worry, we'll cover for you." I rushed home and telephoned Luxembourg. Mr Barnett and I spoke for a while. I thanked him and hung up. Turning towards Martin, who was expectantly watching my every move, I said, "I've got it." We fell into each other's arms and embraced; our lives were about to take a new direction.

They gave me a good send-off at the bank, collecting £200 and giving me the cash, arguing that it would be more useful than a clock or something like that. We said goodbye to our families and prepared to move, both, I suspect, praying that we hadn't made a grave mistake.

I can only imagine what was going through Martin's heart, as we watched the removal van pull away from the home that he'd loved. Great sadness, I think, as it was for me. This was the place where I'd finally laid to rest the ghosts that had haunted me for so many years, and found both love and happiness. Now we were about to take a step together into the unknown, I said a silent prayer as we both climbed into the taxi and headed towards the train that would take us to London and, as promised, our final night in the hotel.

The plane turned in a wide ark, sunlight gleaming off its wings, as it made its final approach towards Luxembourg airport. The date was Friday, 13th June 1980 – a date not lost on either of us. As the *Luxair* jet taxied towards the terminal, I turned towards Martin and smiled, nervously. He looked at me, as if to say, "Well, Dave, here we are. I wonder what the future holds for us both?" At that time, I couldn't have told him. We'd arrived in a whole new life, and a whole new story.

Martin, 1986

Afterword

Our first two years in Luxembourg were difficult. Mart had problems finding work, but this difficulty was eventually resolved and we never, in spite of the initial setbacks, regretted our decision to leave England. In the mid-eighties he sat a examination for the European Parliament and became an English proof-reader, a job that he loves.

As for myself, I finally put the cork firmly back into the bottle and there it's stayed ever since. After working at the Courts of Justice for twenty years, first as a messenger and then as an archivist, I retired on the grounds of ill-health. You see, there's always a price to pay in this life, and my years of drinking finally caught up with me, a long time after the events described in this book.

Do I have any regrets? Yes, of course I do, but there's no point in looking backwards. If by my actions I've harmed anybody in any way, then I can only apologise and ask their forgiveness and let God be my judge.

My story should be seen within the context of its times. I'm often asked if I feel bitter towards the army at my treatment. My answer to that question is no. Why? Because they acted in accordance with military law as it was at that time. To them, I was a criminal. I'm not saying that that's justice, but that's how it was. In January of 2000, homosexuality within the armed forces was no longer regarded as a crime and was decriminalised. Homosexuals were finally able to be treated the same as everyone else and lead their lives without fear –

181

well, at least as far as military law is concerned. To be honest, if I were gay in the armed forces today, it's unlikely that I'd advertise the fact. But at least any young service person who happens to be gay needn't suffer in the way that I did all of those years ago, and for that we should be thankful.

Chris Davies, now a major and still serving, used my case in a lecture he gave to the young soldiers under his command during the change in the law. I remember Chris as a young musician and we served together for many years. I tracked him down a few years ago. He, his wife Rosemary, Martin and I meet up once a year in a European capital city for a reunion and are great friends. Incidentally, they've both recently been awarded the MBE. During his lecture he told his young troops about me and my experiences, and rounded off by saying that Mart and I had been together as a couple for almost thirty years. Afterwards, a number of young servicemen and women came up to him, and asked in amazement, "Sir, has your friend really been with his partner for thirty years?" "Yes, they have," he replied.

On a recent trip to London, I gave a filmed interview telling of my past experiences. A gay group called 'Before-Stonewall' is putting together an archive for future generations; stories of men and women like myself are being recorded before they're lost forever. The interviewer, a highly articulate young man called Mike Upton, asked me as the interview drew to a close if there was one final message that I'd like to give to any young gay person watching the interview in the future. My answer was this, "Don't ever take the freedoms that you have for granted, because there are those out there who would like to take them all away from you."

The debt that I owe to Martin can never be repaid in a thousand lifetimes. At times, I haven't been the easiest person in the world to live with and would be the first person to admit it. Over the years, as I've grown older, and hopefully, just a little wiser, I hope that I've mellowed.

And finally, I thank God that he pointed me in the direction of the *Jester* that cold December night in 1976, for if he hadn't, the ending to this story would have been very different.

I dedicate this book to Martin, with my eternal and undying love.